Praise

for *The Spheres Approach to Happiness and Fulfillment*
and author Garret Biss

"A must have for every library. Garret Biss's approach to managing your 'spheres' will set you free to enjoy the happiness and success that your life deserves."

— STEVE HARRISON, BRADLEY COMMUNICATIONS

"In simple and easy language, [Biss] presents his views on how to find happiness in life, and he is certainly making a lot of sense. This book helps us filter the events going on around us, teaches us how to assess our real circumstances, and shows us the way to handle our personal journeys by utilizing the universal laws. In effect, we can have the power to direct our lives, in spite of the fact that there are things out there that are simply beyond our control. This is a book that will help you fulfill your dreams in life!"

— MARIA BELTRAN, AUTHOR AND PAST CHAIRWOMAN
OF WOMEN IN LITERARY ARTS, INC.

"This short book was long on great advice... [Biss] has clearly done a lot of deep thinking and research into the ills that plague many in today's society, and he has come up with a simplified and easy way for readers to approach their problems, decisions and worries. Any reader who is looking for guidance in dealing with their moods, attitudes, approach or way of living is sure to find excellent advice and direction..."

— TRACY A. FISCHER, AUTHOR OF
THE SORT OF LIFE OF JULIE WINTERFELDT

"*[The Spheres Approach]* by Garret Biss is a self-help book dedicated to the attainment of complete fulfillment through identifying and understanding our passions and desires, and learning to control the outcome of different circumstances and events in our lives. Garret Biss demonstrates the meaning and application of the Seven Universal Laws among other very practical tools. He explains how, through understanding these concepts, we can manage and influence the outcome of the different challenges we face in this dynamic life so as to arrive at the results we desire. Garret Biss aims to help you achieve success without losing sight of what is really important in both your personal and professional life... The message in the book comes from the author's personal experience, and this is very evident from the tone of the writing, making it easier to connect with it. The book also has several exercises and tools aimed at helping you internalize the message so you can apply the knowledge learned to your individual real life circumstances."

— FARIDAH NASSOZI, FREELANCE WRITER

"I found the book to be an excellent guide that will tell readers how to manage their spheres, thereby freeing their minds from the insignificant frustrations in their lives. The author covers the topic extensively and methodically, making it easy for readers to understand and put the advice into practice. Readers can learn how to respond to unfavorable and unpleasant situations and equip ourselves to handle the hardships and struggles that we all face."

— MAMTA MADHAVAN, EDITOR AT GOTPOETRY.COM

"The author's authentic passion for creating a better world is impressive and honorable. So many good ways to give of ourselves. Everyone should read and apply this information!"

— DILYSE DIAZ, LMFT AND AUTHOR

"Garret has mastered the ability to render new insight on an old message."

— STEVE TYSON, COMMISSIONER, CRAVEN COUNTY, NC

"I once spoke with Garret for about an hour and he changed my perspective of life and honestly my happiness, and he's done it again in a few short pages. A must read."

— JUSTIN LOPEZ, U.S. MARINE

"You get out of life what you put into it. By reaching out to others, we gain fulfillment and a sense of purpose. Everyone needs to read this book!"

— TAMMY MORRISON, WEALTH SPECIALIST

"It is so easy to get caught up in the stress and frustrations of life, but sometimes looking outward is the best way to remember that we have so much to offer. I loved this quick, easy read and the motivation it inspired."

— LEAH CAMPBELL, AUTHOR OF *SINGLE INFERTILE FEMALE*

"Now, I realize my purpose! We all have a purpose in this world, and it's obvious that Garret Biss has found his... After reading his book I'm closer to walking in my purpose; he simply explains why we all should give of ourselves in order to make this a better world... Take the opportunity to read this book and your life just simply can't be the same."

— COREY PURDIE, FOUNDER OF WASH AWAY UNEMPLOYMENT
AND MIRACLE WASH NEW BERN

"A refreshingly real read! The time to re-think our approach to living is here and Garret literally challenges us to do so in this quick, life-changing, book. Keeping true to his character as a coach and mentor, Garret doesn't just share his unique philosophy about life, he empowers the reader with summaries to review and actions steps to apply so that every reader can begin to enjoy a happier and more fulfilling life immediately."

- NATHAN HEILMAN, FOUNDER OF ENGAGE [APPAREL]

"Garret takes a very complicated issue and sums it up to provide a thoughtful assessment of our impending reality...."

- TIMOTHY S. DOWNS, DIRECTOR OF ECONOMIC DEVELOPMENT,
CRAVEN COUNTY, NC

"There is a saying, 'The books that help you most are those which make you think the most.' [Garret's] book really got me thinking."

- CINDY BLOT, COMMUNITY AND ECONOMIC DEVELOPMENT MANAGER,
CITY OF NEW BERN, NC

The Spheres
Approach to
Happiness and Fulfillment

GARRET BISS

To my wonderful daughter "KK"

—————————————— ◎ ——————————————

KK, you give purpose to my life. I strive to make the most of myself and my every day with the hope I will inspire you to do the same. The manuscript for this book began as a letter to you; I hope you enjoy it and can make use of the messages I share.

A Life Unchained™

───────── ◎ ─────────

Breaking free from all that holds you back

*I have found that the way I experience life depends upon the thoughts I have and the emotions I feel. When I am angry or upset, everything around me appears negative. When I am happy and content, everything around me seems positive and beautiful. Since it is my choice what I think, it is my choice what emotions I feel. If I can choose my emotions, I can choose the world I see around me. Therefore, it is **my choice** whether my life-experience is a heaven or a hell.*

MANY OF US ARE CURRENTLY experiencing a life that is chained to the confines of conventional wisdom, societal expectations, social norms, and the sometimes best-intended advice of our friends and family. These traditional views imposed on our lives can force us into thinking, believing and acting in ways we are "supposed" to. This approach to life creates unnecessary stress while tempering our dreams and our ambitions, and limiting our perceived ability to achieve the success, joy and happiness we are capable of attaining.

In contrast, *A Life Unchained* approach to existence encompasses a series of personal development and life enrichment philosophies that promise to enable anyone to break free from the chains that keep us from living the dream life we desire and deserve.

The first step to breaking free of these chains is learning the concept of "managing your spheres." *The Spheres Approach to Happiness and Fulfillment* is intended to be an uplifting and empowering message that teaches how to separate ourselves from the stress and negativity that bombards us from the outside world. Once relieved of these negative influences, the Spheres Approach empowers us to overcome the self-effacing thoughts and emotions that come from within.

Harnessing the power of a few fundamental principles, or Universal Laws, can help you to unlock the positive side of every challenge or struggle placed before you. This is a book that reminds us that the most fulfilling and enjoyable life can only be achieved when we learn to be a constant source of love, compassion and positive energy for others. Every word we say and action we take can have an effect on the world around us. When managing our spheres, we ensure that our affect and influence remain positive and uplifting for all involved.

My personal mission as an author and professional speaker is to educate, empower and inspire others toward a happier and more fulfilling life.

Table of Contents

Foreword

––––––––– ◎ –––––––––

Written by Dr. Lea Imsiragic

THIS IS ONE OF THOSE special books that have the power to change your life; it will raise your emotional vibration just by being with you. When you start to read this book, you will experience an instant shift in the way you see and understand the world around you. Garret will help awaken your natural power to think and act in a way that will inspire different feelings, new behaviors and ultimately a different outcome. You will be surprised to find that each time you read from this book, everything around you instantly appears more harmonious and purposeful. My advice is to keep this book close at hand.

The Spheres Approach to Happiness and Fulfillment is a book suitable for everyone. Whether you are a long-time student of happiness and personal growth, or this is your first book in search of a happier and better you, it has something valuable to offer. Garret will teach you fundamental universal laws for enjoying a successful life, and he shares them in a way you can understand and apply right away.

This book will show you fast and easy ways to filter past major life distractions that impede your ability to act from your core being. Garret brings refreshing insight to some ancient wisdom while incorporating many ideas, new for our time. His ability to present a message in such a clear manner will enable any reader to absorb and live these ideas with the first pass through these pages.

Most of all, I personally appreciated the inspiration and positive feeling that this book brought about inside of me with every page. So, let yourself enjoy the direct journey to more peace, greater clarity, and the ability for positive energy to emanate from your natural being. Along this journey, Garret is a wonderful guide.

— DR. LEA IMSIRAGIC

Dr. Imsiragic earned her Master's Degree in the field of magneto biology (human electromagnetical fields) from Medical Faculty Novi Sad, department of Physiology. Dr. Imsiragic's current practice combines knowledge of human physiology with cutting-edge science and practice of energy psychology. She is the author of two books on vibrational healing.

Preface

─────────── ◎ ───────────

I ACTUALLY CAME UP with the concept for *Spheres* during a workout at the Royal Air Force (RAF) gym at Camp Bastion, Afghanistan. I recall a moment of mental clarity I experienced when this idea, a possible answer to something I had been pondering, occurred to me. Fortunately, I was able to find a pencil to scratch out a rudimentary image of the Spheres on a piece of scrap paper before the idea escaped me.

Over the next months in Afghanistan, I reflected on this concept of Spheres. I was determined to figure out how it was meaningful. I kept a journal of the thoughts and connections I made that fell like puzzle pieces into this *Spheres* concept. The first draft of this manuscript was born.

When I first attempted to capture in words what I saw for a moment in my mind, the entirety of my understanding was about the size of a single blog post. For the next three years, I continued to reflect on the Spheres, and the connections and clarity this concept brought to many ideas and lessons I had been exposed to previously.

I spent a lot of time during this deployment in 2013 reading through self-help books and watching seminar videos from Bob

Proctor, Jack Canfield, Napoleon Hill, Jim Rohn, and others. I watched TED videos and attended various chapel services with pen and paper in hand. I was no stranger to the many philosophies about happiness and life fulfillment, but the exposure to this material didn't allow me to cultivate a life experience that felt as happy or fulfilling as I believed it should; there had to be an answer somewhere.

I spent months reflecting on the similarities between the varying life philosophies—the positive mental attitude ideas and techniques they each presented. Each book I read presented various ways to deal with or move beyond the "negative" things that occur in our life. While I had been armed with some great ideas, and now had many techniques in my toolbox, I wasn't able to apply them in my life to create the effect I desired. Spheres gave me hope—a possible answer by changing the context of how my positive mental attitude was applied.

The tools and techniques shared with me by the Rohns and Canfields of the world may enable others to find happiness and success in their lives, but only if applied in the right context. When I tried to reflect on all the happenings of the world in a positive way—the far-off things, the near and personal things, the big things, the little things—I felt overwhelmed and became exhausted. While all the advice on finding and living a positive, happy life made sense, I wasn't able to create the feeling of happiness, purpose and satisfaction I desired.

After some great reflection, it dawned on me: I was worrying about too many things that had no relevance to me. I was allowing a flow of negative and irrelevant energy into my life. My mind was inundated with "all the stuff," and it made it hard to focus on "the important stuff."

We didn't have much access to TV in Afghanistan. In fact, anything we had was either a prerecorded show someone brought with them from home or one of the few news stations we were able to stream on our computers. One recollection I have that led to this philosophy of Spheres was the news of a chemical factory explosion somewhere in the Midwest during my deployment. I noticed that nearly every office I walked into for a few days had the news streaming on at least one computer. All the reporters talked about was the destruction, devastation, loss of life and sadness that came from this tragic event. In good 24-hour news broadcast fashion, they did not shut up about it for almost a week.

With little else to distract them, I watched many coworkers staring at the news stream in fascination, like moths to a flame. This touching but very tragic story was a constant feed of negative energy into each viewer's mind, feeding their conscious and unconscious thoughts and taking an apparent toll on everyone's now somber and deflated moods.

This factory explosion occurred about the same time I was reading and listening to some work by Napoleon Hill. In this material, Hill was discussing the relationship between emotional vibration and the thoughts and ideas we allow into our minds. Our thoughts, Hill taught, whether good or bad, affect our emotions. These emotions, in turn, affect our thoughts, mood, actions and even our health.

At this time, I was beginning to piece Hill's philosophy together with the addictive stream of negative news we were being bombarded with. I began trying to reconcile it with the ideas I was hearing about maintaining a positive mental attitude.

And that was when I began to realize that the negative stream of news we were being exposed to had absolutely no bearing on any one of our lives in Afghanistan. With that realization, I determined that I could either expend energy trying to spin these negatives that didn't actually affect me into positives, or I could simply turn off the TV and stop this source of negative thoughts completely.

I began to see this action of turning off the news as a metaphor for dealing with everything that doesn't affect me. The news was no different than gossip between others, events going on thousands of miles away, or the seemingly constant stream of thoughts dedicated to a past I could no longer change or affect. Each of these things was a source of negative thoughts, which I now knew were a direct contributor to my emotional state. Instead of using what I knew about the Universal Laws to find positive thoughts and inspiration to combat these negative things on my mind, I realized I should treat them all like the news—just turn them off.

For some reason, I found myself, as many others do, conditioned to take comfort in dwelling on negative things. It sometimes makes us feel better to think we are victims of circumstances and just doing the best we can. When our professional life isn't going well, it is easy to blame the bad economy. When our finances are out of whack, we blame the tax situation. When we can't get a loan, we blame the government. But all of these excuses have just one major flaw—they are just excuses. Not reality.

People in every kind of economy, good and bad, are getting rich. It's not the conditions out there that affect what we are or who we become; it's the circumstances much closer to home and the actions we take in spite of those conditions, not because of them, that make the difference.

This analogy of the world and its Spheres began as I pieced these thoughts together. I realized there is only so much of the world around me that I can truly affect or influence. There is only so much of the world that truly affects my life experience. Does an unemployment rate increase affect me if I currently have a job in the military? Nope. Does a falling stock market affect my life if I don't own any stocks? Nope. Can I do something to change what the President is planning to do with foreign policy? Not likely. When I have the opportunity, I can vote for politicians who will address these problems and bring about change, but, other than that, I can't personally bring about change.

So why live as though all these far-off things affect me? Why allow the negative emotions they inspire into my life?

Why let them steal my attention from something right before me that I can affect and influence, like my relationship with my daughter? Or how hard I work? Or the way I treat others around me?

That was the image that came to my mind somewhere between the dumbbell rack and the cable machine at the gym in Afghanistan. I ran to the corner and scratched out some notes on a notepad—the vision that would eventually become this book.

What makes my message different from all the other messages about positive thinking out there? Many of the ideas I discuss have been taught by others and shared for centuries. But it can get overwhelming to think of it all on that broad spectrum. To me, it is applying these ideas in the context of Spheres segregation that makes the difference.

Many thoughts and ideas will be shared in this book. Every reader will understand or experience the information and ideas a little differently; each will get something unique from the text. If you think the information is interesting, but nothing really strikes you as something that might help in your circumstances, then I appreciate your interest and your willingness to simply give it a read. If someday you meet someone who may benefit from these ideas, I hope you will share the book with them.

If, on the other hand, you think there are some ideas and insights that have come from this book that would be of great benefit to you, I am honored by the privilege to share these thoughts. I recommend you not make this your last reading of this book.

If you want to get the most from these ideas and find a way to incorporate them into your life and your thinking, then be sure to pick up this book again and read it over at least one more time. Maybe you could let the ideas sink in for a few days or weeks and then give the text another read.

Next time through, try to read just one section at a time with a few days to digest and implement the ideas from that section before reading the next. Before long, the thoughts and ideas we will discuss here will take on a life of their own for you. The more you try out a few of these concepts, the more they will become a part of who you are. Maybe you won't see the world or use these tools in the same way that I do, but you will see things in a way that helps make your life a little better, your experience a little brighter.

What more can we want from life?

Section One:
The Basics

Chapter 1

○

What do I mean by "Spheres?"

I ENVISION THE WORLD as being comprised of three concentric spheres. You might picture these three spheres as concentric bubbles.

The largest sphere, which I think of as the **Indirect Sphere,** encompasses everything that happens in the world, good or bad, that does not directly affect us. This might include things such as news of an occurrence a thousand miles away or word of a tragedy happening overseas. Perhaps a classmate from high school, whom you haven't spoken to in years, recently got married or lost a job. Maybe a well-known celebrity you like lost a child.

We hear about these things often, and though they don't affect us directly, they can have an impact on us—if we allow them to. If we ponder or ruminate over these indirect occurrences, they can affect our mood, our concentration, and ultimately, the actions we take, which will have a direct effect on the results we experience.

The next sphere, what I call the **Direct Sphere**, encompasses all the things and events in this world that do directly affect us. This could be the weather outside today, the current state of our finances, or the traffic we encounter on our way to work. While each of these things has a direct impact on us, I have found that it is entirely up to us to determine what that impact is and how we react to it.

Does the traffic we encounter infuriate us, or do we embrace the opportunity to disconnect? Does the heavy rain on our only day off ruin our mood, or do we allow it to inspire us to find a productive indoor activity? We cannot control what happens within this Direct Sphere, but we can control how we respond to those occurrences.

The last sphere, the **Action Sphere**, includes all that we can impact in the world with our own lives. This sphere extends beyond us as we interact with the world through our words and actions; it resides within us in the thoughts and self-talk we allow in our minds.

Is there anyone among us who couldn't benefit from a few extra hours in their day—additional time and energy to attend to the many things vying for our attention? Whether we would spend that time relaxing with friends, or cleaning up the endless to-do list we harbor in the back of our minds, each of us could surely find a productive way to invest a few extra hours (and the energy those hours would require) if we had them.

The good news is that extra time and energy are actually ours to find. When we identify the things in the world around us that do not directly affect us but have been weighing on our minds, we can remove those distractions and negative influences. We can regain our attention to invest in the things that matter most.

It can be enjoyable to indulge in the negative events shared on the news, to ruminate with friends about all the things going wrong in our lives, or to be "in the know" about the latest happenings in Hollywood or tragedies overseas. But if these distractions prevent us from attending to things within our own bubble, the things that can bring us the greatest joy or sense of purpose, are they worth it?

We each experience frustrations and challenges throughout our lives. We fail to get a promotion, we have a car accident, our refrigerator breaks or we have an argument with a friend. Each of these things has a direct impact on us. By managing our Spheres, we hold a lens to these challenges, allowing ourselves to find the opportunities or benefits that are presented by every event or circumstance in our lives. This analysis equips us with something good to focus on, and it allows us to regain our attention from the frustrations we face.

By managing our Spheres, we aim to reduce the negative energy and distractions that come into our lives. Through this process, we first cut off the flow of negative energy and negatively inspired thoughts brought on by the many things that do not directly affect us. We then manage everything in our lives that does have a direct influence by using various tools or techniques that allow us to identify and focus on the positive things taking place around us. In doing this, we free our minds and attention from the anguish of ruminating on the problems or "bad luck" we experience.

But that isn't all. By managing our spheres, we also learn that we are able to control the impact we have on the world around us. Don't we all want to know that we have had a positive impact on the life of someone else? Whether a child or a friend, it is incredibly validating to know another person's life is better because of our existence. Nobody wants to lie on their deathbed and feel as though they have done nothing to make the world a better place.

Unfortunately, in the busyness of life, we are often caught up in the moment and can miss the brashness we exhibit toward others or the lack of care and attention we show to those dearest to us. By managing our spheres, we work to share the best of ourselves with those around us—we ensure our direct and indirect impact on the world is a positive one.

I am excited to take a journey with you, sharing what I have learned about the benefits of managing our spheres over the years. I have found that by managing these three spheres in my own life, I have drastically reduced the stress and negative energy that once overwhelmed me. I still face all the usual struggles and challenges we all come up against, but now, instead of life's challenges knocking me down, I take the bump and keep on charging. By managing my spheres, I have freed my mind from many of the insignificant frustrations that once plagued me. I have opened myself up to investing that regained time and energy into what I enjoy most in life, which has put me on a much happier path toward a more successful future.

This is what I want for you, as well.

Events and Circumstances

I WILL MAKE REGULAR REFERENCES to both the events and circumstances that occur in our lives. Often, I will talk about events and circumstances concurrently because they can each affect us in the same way, and we can respond to both with the same actions or thought processes.

The events and circumstances in our lives are what guide us

along the road we travel. That said, events and circumstances are two very different things.

By **Event,** I mean anything that may happen to us, either directly or indirectly. An event has occurred in the past or is presently taking place. It may also be something that we expect to occur in the future, which is affecting our emotions today. An event could be the fire that burned your house down, the accident that caused traffic to back up, or the hurtful words that someone shared with you. An event can also be the things that occur in the world around us: the murder that happened the next town over or the storm that is brewing a state away.

Events aren't always negative; every positive thing that happens is also an event. The scratch-off ticket that just won you $50, the great dinner you just enjoyed, or the cheerful phone call from a good friend—these are all events.

A **Circumstance,** on the other hand, is some characteristic about the state of your life, or the world you experience. A circumstance may be that you are now homeless, that you have an abusive friend in your life, or that you are late for work. Circumstances may be the result of actions taken over a long period of time. If you are extremely wealthy or devastatingly poor, those are circumstances. If you are in great health or significantly obese, those are also circumstances. If you suffer from a condition such as post-traumatic stress or an addiction such as alcoholism, that condition is a circumstance of the life you experience.

When a circumstance brings negative energy into your life, you can use the ideas we will discuss to correct the negative energy and start drawing positive energy from the seemingly negative circumstance.

Past events often create the circumstances we encounter today.

Events may have transpired at work, for instance, which culminated in you losing your job. Your current circumstance is that you are now unemployed. Events that happen beyond our control create the outside circumstances we encounter as well. For instance, actions taken by others in the government or on Wall Street may affect the economy in your town or the industry in which you now work.

The Power Within

FROM AN EARLY AGE, we begin to see and remember things in the world that condition the way we understand life. We face experiences that result in specific outcomes. After repeated exposure, we are conditioned to understand that certain events and circumstances create certain results. With this information, we make assumptions about how other events and circumstances will manifest results or outcomes in our lives. We learn from our personal experiences, the experiences of our friends and colleagues, and the experiences of others on television or in the books we read. The collection of these experiences and observations begin to condition our minds to expect certain outcomes when certain inputs occur.

Through the common conditioning we receive with this life experience, or sometimes through the well-intended advice of others, we find it natural to look at reasons beyond our control for the cause of our unhappiness and struggles. We may also tend to look outside ourselves for our own personal happiness. The things we buy, the places we go, the people we associate with—we assume all of these things are supposed to make us happy. And, if we are not happy, we may feel that it is because of someone or something else.

Only with time, great teachers and significant reflection, have I learned the massive fallacy in this line of thinking.

> *"A man is about as happy as he makes up his mind to be."*
> — ABRAHAM LINCOLN

The truth that many people eventually come to understand is that happiness only comes from within. As Lincoln points out, our happiness is up to us and is created by our chosen state of mind. No amount of success or abundance of any form will create happiness if you don't build the proper emotional foundation and develop that source of happiness from within. With just a little reflection and the learning of a few ideas, it is easy to develop and appreciate this vital truth about life. It doesn't take long to flip a switch in our mind and to understand that the truest source for our own happiness and satisfaction lies within us.

Our Life, The Movie

I AM A HUGE FAN of going to the movies. I cherish the opportunity to escape from my day and to journey into the lives of others through a movie experience. I love the way some movies touch me. I enjoy the happiness I feel for the characters I don't know. I appreciate the inspiration I feel and the great ideas I sometimes learn.

On occasion, I watch movies where characters face dire circumstances, and the movie ends in tragedy. In a way, this can make me feel better about my own, comparatively easy life. Sometimes my own struggles and faults appear trivial, if only for a moment, after I see what others may have faced.

Other times, I may see the story of a person who overcomes severe odds and difficult challenges while still achieving amazing results. This can inspire me to keep at my own struggles and to find a way to succeed, no matter how difficult the situation I currently face may seem.

What I find incredible is how much an experience at the movies can touch us and affect our emotions. We go into the theatre well aware that what we are about to see is complete fiction. We see on the screen before us actors and actresses that we have seen in many other films. There is no mistake in our mind that these people are just pretending because we have seen them play other fictitious characters before. Yet with all this in our mind, we still experience an emotional roller coaster and find ourselves influenced by the movie experience.

We feel sad, we feel happy, we feel moments of love, of sorrow, hope or anger. This fictitious story, which has no actual relevance in our lives, can touch our hearts or enrage our minds. We may even shed a tear. If we are watching a good thriller, we may fear for our own lives as our senses are heightened and the adrenaline begins pumping, just the same as if we were running for our lives in reality.

While we are at the movies, as we begin to feel an emotional reaction like anger or rage toward the story on the screen, we could easily stop this reaction by telling ourselves the movie isn't real. If we are watching a horror movie where Freddy or Jason is about to take another victim, we can stop our emotional reactions—the fear and adrenaline rushing through our body—by reminding ourselves it is just a movie. Nothing on the screen actually affects us or threatens our body. We may even remind ourselves of this while we are covering our eyes so we don't continue to stimulate those emotions. If we choose not to see the screen, it will no longer inspire the same fear.

Once we walk away from the theatre and return to our reality, we remember the story was fictitious, and the emotions soon fade. Often, the moment we return to the hustle and bustle of our lives, we forget how we were touched or inspired. The movie's influence on our hearts and minds soon vanishes. The inspiration that we may have felt begins to fade when we remember our own challenges or hurdles; challenges and hurdles the characters on screen didn't have to face. The love or hope we held for a moment dissipates when we are once again reminded of our own personal struggles and fears.

Unfortunately, the positive emotions or inspiration we may have felt while viewing a movie often fade the quickest. It is easy to find all the reasons *our* life won't work out as beautifully as the one we just watched on screen. The first phone call or conversation you experience may be enough to reverse the positive energy from your imaginary journey—if you let it.

Negative emotions that come from these fictitious experiences tend to linger a bit longer. The thoughts and ideas that reinforce our fears and stimulate anxiety may last for days, if not weeks. After watching a good thriller, perhaps the latest *Paranormal Activity*, we may find ourselves sleeping with an extra light on, checking the door locks one more time before bed, and taking one more look in the closets before going to sleep. I remember as a kid, after watching a scary movie, I was startled for weeks. I would run and jump as far as I could to get in bed so that my feet were never within reach of any potential monster underneath.

While we may have a better grasp of reality as adults, it doesn't mean those fears don't linger.

In our real lives, there are many things we see that we allow to affect us the same as a movie might. We hear stories that don't actually touch our lives, but that can inspire, anger, or depress us. We hear about a typhoon happening 6,000 miles away or a tornado in a neighboring state, and we are stirred to emotion. We find ourselves inspired by stories of heroism and selfless generosity as others help the victims recover.

The images that flash through our mind may frighten us, shock us, or later inspire us and warm our hearts. However, like the effect we get from the movies, many times it is the negative emotions that we carry with us longer. The depression, anxiety and fear that are inspired by the storm or a recent tragedy can fester much longer in our minds than the stories of hope. If not in our conscious thoughts, these ideas may linger in our subconscious in ways we don't realize. We may feel a little bit saddened, or a little less energetic and inspired. We may lose our drive, without really understanding why.

The Reaction is Yours to Control

WE TEND TO ALLOW things like violence on TV, drama in movies, and traumatic stories on the news to affect our emotions. Most of us have experienced dissatisfaction, anxiety and unhappiness in our lives. Often, this negative emotional energy originates from sources beyond our control. This response we have takes a toll, though. While we can't always control the events and circumstances that may lead to negative energy, we can control the way we respond to those events in our lives.

If we didn't have control over the way we reacted to things in life, then every event or circumstance would affect each person in exactly the same way. We know this isn't true because every victim of a particular tragedy does not respond identically. Everyone blessed with the same gifts does not create the same future.

The way we have each been conditioned to respond through our own unique personal history and prior experiences is a significant factor that determines how certain future events will affect us. For example, a mother may react differently to news stories of a school shooting than a teenager would. A person who lost a home to a fire will likely react differently to news of wildfires than someone who has never shared a similar experience.

While conditioning does play a role in how events touch us, our physical and emotional response is actually controlled by how we choose to evaluate and react—we determine how deeply life events will affect us. Just like in the movies, the person who covers their eyes during a scary segment of a thriller will have a different emotional response than the person who doesn't. Those who remind themselves that a movie is fictional when there is a horrific war scene or an exhilarating chase won't feel the same emotional effect as those who allow themselves to become absorbed in the story.

Obviously, we know from experience this isn't how things work; everyone responds to the events in their lives differently. But we need to understand why so that we can appreciate the true empowerment of controlling our own reactions.

In the pages to come, we will discuss how we can view, filter and manage the events and circumstances that occur in our lives so that we can choose how our mind and body responds. When tragic or negative things happen beyond our control, particularly when they have little relevance to our lives, we will find ways to "cover our eyes" from these events so we don't embark on the negative emotional roller coaster. I am not suggesting that we pretend bad things don't exist around us. I am only suggesting that we not fixate on things we are not directly affected by and have no control over.

Life has as much beauty, happiness and positive energy as it does despair and frustration. By choosing when to peer closely (or become engulfed in a life experience) and when to look away, you decide whether the life you experience is a drama, a love story, a comedy or a thriller.

We will discuss ways to see things in life the way we want to see them by using a process similar to the one we use when we remind ourselves a movie is fictional in order to condition the emotional response we have.

As we live each day, we aren't just witnessing the world around us. We are also creating a movie at the same time—a movie of life experience. We are directing many of the events and circumstances in our own world. If we were directing a movie that was to be our life, we would want the happiest and most abundant life we could create. In Spheres, we will discuss the ways your responses to the world around you can create that life you desire.

Chapter 2

—————————— ◎ ——————————

The Universal Laws

EVERY EVENT AND CIRCUMSTANCE in life can be viewed through the lens of seven Universal Laws (ULs). Just as every color we see is some combination of red, yellow and blue, everything that happens in our lives can be seen as a combination of these seven ULs at work. Through the lenses of these ULs, we can find reason, purpose and a positive consequence of every challenge or struggle we may have faced.

These aren't new concepts. Much of the philosophy surrounding the ULs has been taught since the beginning of time. Once you understand the ULs, you will find traces of their mention everywhere you look, if not by name, then by principle or concept. I now understand that every deemed "truth," pearl of wisdom, or piece of sage advice (be it a famous quote or a religious teaching) boils down to a discussion of these seven Universal Laws at work. They are everywhere!

Universal Laws are tools that we can use to see the blessings in every life experience. Just as arithmetic allows us to add and subtract numbers to manage our time and finances, the Universal Laws can allow us to see the positive side of even the most negative experiences. Sometimes, the positive aspect of things does not outweigh the anguish and frustration in our minds, but seeing that small silver lining amidst our struggles does make things easier to deal with.

Depending on what you read, you may find information on as many as 21 different Universal Laws. For the purposes of this book, we will talk specifically about what I view to be the seven primary Universal Laws. After reflecting on the disparity of these "extra" laws, I have come to perceive them to be merely combinations of, or special cases for, the selected laws we will discuss. Just as every color under the sun can be created with a combination of the three primary colors, all additional ULs have a foundation in these primary seven.

The ULs we will discuss are The Law of Vibration, The Law of Relativity, The Law of Polarity, The Law of Cause and Effect, The Law of Rhythm, The Law of Gender, and The Law of Transmutation of Energy.

The Law Of Vibration

THE LAW OF VIBRATION is the most vital Law to understand for the management of our Spheres and our ability to live the life we desire. This Law presents the truth that everything in the Universe is made up of energy that vibrates at a certain frequency. The vibrational frequency of physical objects gives each its unique physical properties. Solid objects vibrate at a much slower rate than liquids or gases. Warmer objects are vibrating faster than cold objects. When you look at an object, the color you see is created by the frequency of light reflecting off that object. Frequency is simply a rate of vibration.

Our emotions are also a kind of vibration. At any given moment, you are producing an emotional, vibrational frequency. When you feel love, appreciation, compassion or hope, all these emotions make you feel good inside—they give you a positive vibration. Conversely, the bad feelings within you when you're feeling depressed, angry, or hateful are all negative emotional vibrations.

The Law of Vibration describes that in a metaphysical sense, objects of a similar vibration are attracted to one another. Positive emotions inspire and perpetuate other positive emotions, just as negative emotions like fear and anxiety can bring about other negative emotions. This spread of emotions does not just occur within us, but our emotions can spread to those around us. A grumpy person can spread their negative mood, and a positive and optimistic person can inspire those same feelings in another. We tend to feel best around people who are in the same vibration as we are at the moment. "Birds of a feather flock together."

Not only do emotional vibrations attract similar vibrations; they are repelled by the opposite. At times when you are shining with positive feelings, don't negative and complaining people seem annoying? And when you are in a funk and feeling pity for yourself, running into a happy and positive person can be frustrating.

The emotional energy we feel inside and emit to our environment through our words and actions has a way of conditioning our perspective. When our day starts out on a bad note, or troubling things in our life are piling up, it becomes easy to spot many of the other "bad" things going on. When you have one negative event occur in your day, it can spark a landslide of other negative events and circumstances. This occurs because the negative emotional energy you emit attracts negative thoughts and manifestations to your experience. "When it rains, it pours."

When we are in a funk or when we are feeling very upbeat and positive, we have a tendency to want to be around people who are feeling the same emotions. Negative energy and emotions in people attract others in a similar state. If downtrodden and frustrated with things at the office, we congregate with others holding the same outlook. When you find yourself in a bad mood, it often feels like everyone around you is in a bad mood or has negative things happening to them as well. "Misery loves company."

Alternatively, when feeling upbeat, excited and optimistic, we are not just attracted to people feeling similar emotions, but we can even excite or illicit these emotions in others who aren't at that positive emotional state.

There are plenty of clichéd quotes devoted to exactly this phenomenon—because whether it is acknowledged as the Law of Vibration or not, this is something we all witness every day.

The Law of Vibration has many implications, but the key is to appreciate that vibrations of a certain type, whether positive or negative, welcome into your life more physical and emotional manifestations of that same type.

We must protect ourselves from negative emotional vibrations because these feelings make it hard to see the many good and wondrous things that are going well in our lives. Failing to focus on positive things in the world, and instead seeing the bad and associating with similarly sour people, leads to a downward spiral of emotional energy. The worse you feel emotionally, the less you feel inspired to take actions that may improve a bad situation. Negative thoughts and emotions taint our perception and temper our drive to create a better situation, or even to believe that a better situation is possible.

Fortunately, when you feel great and are swelling with positive emotions like love, confidence, and compassion, you see and act upon other positive and inspiring things around you. When you demonstrate to those around you particularly positive emotions, you attract friendships and interactions with people of a similar upbeat emotional vibration and outlook. The confidence and optimistic drive that good emotions create lead us to the constructive actions that propel us forward. The actions we take when in a positive vibration help attract more good things to our life—easy breaks, fortune, advancement, promotions, adventure, prosperity, and the list goes on.

This chain of positive manifestation begins with the positive emotional vibrations, making this Law of Vibration the most important to grasp. When we feel negative emotions and things aren't happening in our life as we may like, the quickest solution is to change our emotional vibration, thus changing the tides of our physical world.

You may have read *The Secret* by Rhonda Burns or seen the movie. In *The Secret*, it is suggested that we attract physical manifestations into our life with the thoughts and images we hold in our mind. This is true not just for good experiences, but also for bad ones.

President Abraham Lincoln once shared the insight that, "When I do good, I feel good. When I do bad, I feel bad."

To continue this train of thought, when we feel good, we are inspired and positive. When we're inspired and positive, we take action that brings good things to our life. The actual "doing," which includes thinking, feeling, visualizing and acting, is what starts the process.

Positive thoughts produce positive vibrations; positive vibrations produce positive results. So, planting the seed for the life of happiness and fulfillment you desire begins with your thoughts.

You see, most of us have had it backwards. **Happiness, joy, and a sense of fulfillment are not the result of success or accomplishment. Instead, functioning from a state of happiness, gratitude, and spreading love and joy in the Universe can help you achieve success, fulfillment, abundance and prosperity.**

Our discussion begins with the Law of Vibration because maintaining a positive vibration is central to finding happiness and success. The other Universal Laws (ULs) can be used as tools to "protect your vibration" and to keep your thoughts and feelings positive. The other ULs help us to accept and appreciate every event and circumstance in our life, even the bad ones, and help us deal with any regret, frustration or anger by transforming those negative emotions/vibrations to positive thoughts.

A Quick Tip for Vibration: You cannot experience both a positive and negative emotional vibration at the same time. We may alternate back and forth very quickly as we recall different thoughts, but a negative thought or emotion cannot linger when a positive one replaces it. Gratitude can be a great tool for finding a positive thought and moving you to a positive emotional vibration from a negative one. Whenever you feel yourself tending toward or harboring a negative emotional vibration, stop and think of a few things you have to be grateful for. Be grateful for the simple things you have, like the clothes on your back, the air in your lungs, the ground beneath your feet. Or be grateful for the important things in life such as the experiences you have had, the friends in your life or the successes you've known. If you can't think of anything you have to be grateful for at the moment, think of a few negative things you can be grateful you don't have. Be grateful that you do not have a headache, a bad cold or an open wound. Establish this feeling of gratitude, and it will replace the negative emotions on your mind.

The Law Of Relativity

When we change the way we look at things,
The things we look at change.

— DR. WAYNE DYER

I AM SURE YOU HAVE HEARD about Einstein's Theory of Relativity, the one that basically says the perceived reality of everything that happens in the world is relative to the person or observer who views the event. In a metaphysical sense, this breaks down more simply to mean that whether an event is deemed to be good or bad depends on who is observing it and where they are emotionally when the event occurs. More simply, nothing is either "good" or "bad" until you have a reference point to relate it to something else.

For us to have the thought that something in our life is bad or unpleasant, we must know something better to compare it to. If we walk outside on a cold summer morning, and we think to ourselves "this is cold," we are comparing the weather (a relative value) to a morning that was warmer. When a person is rude to us, we only know they were rude because we have other experiences of people being nice. If we are having a bad day, we only know it is bad because we are able to compare it to good days we have had in the past.

Let's say you have been working around your office for a few hours when you begin to feel a little thirsty. Your slight thirst isn't bothersome, but you figure it is a good excuse to take a break from what you are doing to find something to drink. After a few moments of looking around, all you come up with is lukewarm water from a day-old bottle on your desk. The prospect of drinking this water isn't nearly appealing enough, so you choose to go on being thirsty for a while longer until you can get something else.

But what if you had just finished running a 10k race and crossed the finish line utterly parched? If you felt as though you could hardly take another step until you found something to quench your dire thirst, wouldn't that same bottle of water from your office suddenly seem more appealing?

Now, imagine you have been stranded on a deserted island for the last week. You've hardly had enough water to survive, and your last sip was a few days ago. You fear that if you don't find something to drink very soon, your death will be imminent. Don't you imagine that at this point, finding the same lukewarm bottle of water would seem like a wonderful and positive event?

The water, of course, is not inherently good or bad. Whatever you perceive it to be is relative to your situation and the way you choose to think about it.

We can use this Law as a tool to protect our vibration by **viewing the negative circumstances or events in our life through the lens of something worse.**

Not too long ago, I was driving to work when I encountered unusually heavy traffic—backed up for more than a mile. As a result of this traffic, I was most certainly going to be late to work.

I think most people who have experienced a similar situation can relate to the growing frustration I was feeling in that moment. There was rain pouring down, everyone was driving slowly, and all I could do was watch the clock tick by, knowing that I was becoming later by the minute.

Just as I really started to feel infuriated by the situation, I recognized my thoughts and realized I was only getting upset because I could remember a bright and sunny morning driving to work when there had been no traffic. I was frustrated because everything wasn't going as smoothly as it had in the past, and I was allowing that to affect my mood and attitude.

Applying this Law of Relativity to protect my vibration, I tried to imagine a situation that would be worse. As I approached the next intersection, I saw a car that was stuck on the side of the road. When I got closer, I could see that the vehicle had a flat tire and the driver was out in the pouring, cold rain working to change it. I immediately became grateful that I was warm and dry inside my vehicle. Yes, I was going to be a few minutes late for work, but I wasn't soaking wet and cold like this poor guy. My circumstances seemed pretty good relative to the other driver; things certainly could have been much worse.

One trick to applying this Law is that I didn't have to see someone experiencing a worse situation in order to make mine relatively better. Had I never seen that car on the side of the road, I could have just imagined a way that my current circumstances were better than an alternative. That would have had the same effect. For instance, I could have been involved in a car accident. Or running late for a meeting that was critical to the advancement of my career. Or dealing with a car that had broken down in the middle of the road. Relatively speaking, running a few minutes late for work was a better alternative to all of those possibilities.

Thoughts of gratitude, in many ways, are just an application of relativity. When we are grateful for something we have, it is because we are comparing it to something that we know that is worse. While stuck in traffic and late for work, I improved my state of mind by thinking of things I was grateful for in the moment, like my safe, dry, warm vehicle. I was appreciative, and immediately the traffic seemed like only a minor inconvenience, not a plot against me.

Quick Tip for Relativity: It can be helpful to have a few "go-to" bad situations in the back of your mind when you're working with the Law of Relativity. I have one experience during my Marine Corps training that is possibly the worst physical experience I can recall. That day was about 10 degrees below freezing on the surface, but some strange metrological condition made it warmer in the clouds overhead. This warmer temperature in the clouds meant buckets of rain dumping on me the entire day. Some rain froze the instant it hit my clothes; other raindrops caught in my saturated hat and collar then dripped down my neck and under my shirt. Fourteen hours of running through the woods, lying on the frozen ground, and hiking for miles was not a fun time. (How nobody lost a digit to frostbite or experienced hypothermia that day is still a mystery to me.) This experience is now one I have on instant recall any time I face a little rain on a cold winter day. Nothing is as bad as that day of Marine training.

Maybe you have a few particularly horrible memories of physical, emotional, financial or even spiritual turmoil that you have faced. Recall one of these times when you face a challenging situation. Remember, relative to the worst of times, your challenge today isn't all that bad.

The Law Of Polarity

A CCORDING TO THE LAW OF POLARITY, every "good" thing that occurs in the Universe also comes accompanied by an equal but opposite "bad." Likewise, for every bad event, there is an equal but opposite good that is created. Just as Newton taught us, "For every action, there is an equal and opposite reaction." That is polarity.

So the Law of Relativity says that nothing is either good or bad until you relate it to something else. And the Law of Polarity states that with every good comes an equal and opposite bad, or vice versa. Whether the number 1,000 is big or small depends on what you compare it to—its relativity. But the fact that 1,000 exists means that -1,000 also exists. That's polarity.

If you examine an experience in your life, all the good that comes from that experience coexists with an equal sum of negative circumstances that event created. Think of doing a very strenuous physical exercise. All the pain and discomfort you experience during the exercise, whether it's weight training or a long, hard run, is balanced by the positive benefits to your health and emotional wellness once the workout is complete. The greater the pain, the greater the gain, so they say.

Similarly, all the mental, emotional and psychological discomfort you felt while going through school is balanced by the benefits to your education and future opportunities. A college degree is many times more challenging than a high school diploma, but the rewards are equally greater for those willing to pursue that higher education.

Understanding the Law of Polarity is great for putting things into perspective. When we face a challenge or a difficult time, we

know there is some equal good awaiting us. We also understand that too much easy living or relaxing comes at a cost.

Still, it can sometimes be difficult to see the potential good when in the middle of those darker challenges. I have a friend, Leah Campbell, who at a young age was diagnosed with an illness that left her in a great deal of physical pain and eventually stripped her of her fertility. She's written a book of her own, *Single Infertile Female*, so I won't give too many of the details away here, but needless to say, she went through a dark period, feeling let down by her body and stripped of the one dream she had always harbored, that of motherhood.

Her book is a look back at those years, the times when she felt the most let down by life and unsure of where she was even supposed to look next. It is clear she often couldn't comprehend there being any possible good to this devastating turn of events in her life. She felt lost, alone and broken down.

It was during the years that followed this darkest time that Leah began to experience the equal good that accompanies every bad. Turning to writing as a resource for healing, she was able to become an advocate for others suffering from the same disease she had. She raised awareness and spread education while also getting enough attention for her writing to eventually make that her full-time career—a lifelong dream she had never previously believed possible. And, just when she had given up hope of ever fulfilling her dream of motherhood, a serendipitous series of events led to her surprise adoption of a beautiful little girl—a daughter she now says was worth every ounce of heartache to get to.

More than once, Leah has told me that looking back on that series of events has served as her reminder of the Law of Polarity at work in every new set of challenges she has faced. Knowing that there is always an equal and opposite good for every bad helps her to forge ahead, even when life is at its toughest.

Understanding the Law of Polarity can be incredibly valuable when dealing with life's struggles. But it can also serve to keep you grounded when life is good.

Consider an experience from your own life that was particularly wonderful. Maybe you had an opportunity to take a vacation, experience a unique time with a friend or meet someone new. These occurrences serve as the brightest spots in our lives. Still, every wonderful experience you enjoy comes at the cost of something else. The time you spend with friends or trying something new (the positive) is time that you cannot invest in something else—perhaps visiting with a relative, or working toward a future goal. Sure, taking advantage of a unique opportunity at work or a chance to travel is certainly worthwhile, but the time it takes prevents you from pursuing another, possibly more rewarding experience. There is always a give and take. Enjoy your positive experiences to the fullest without regret. Make the most of your high points, but appreciate the costs that made those highs possible.

Applying this idea to the world as we experience it, you can see that every opportunity comes with some level of sacrifice, and every failure brings a new prospect or valuable experience.

> *"Every experience, no matter how bad it seems,*
> *holds within it a blessing of the same kind.*
> *The goal is to find it!"*
> — BUDDHA

The Law of Polarity is particularly useful when we are attempting to relate to other people. Occasionally in life, we will come across mean, nasty, negative people. There will also be times when our experiences with a certain person aren't necessarily as extreme, yet we just can't seem to meet eye to eye with someone we need to work with. In each of these situations, the Law of Polarity is at work.

When I am having a hard time getting along with someone, I often remind myself of the quote by Ralph Waldo Emerson, "In my walks, every man I meet is my superior in some way; in that, I can learn from him." This point reminds me that no matter how hard a time I have relating to another person, there is something in him or her that is good; something I can respect. And in some way, they are better than me at something, which means that I can always learn from them and gain something from our inter-actions.

If I can find that one thing I respect, or if I can see something from their point of view that I may be able to relate to, then I can focus on that one thing, making the rest of our relationship much more positive. You don't have to like or agree with everything about someone, but if you can just find one or two small things, it makes the rest easier.

Abraham Lincoln is rumored to have once said, "I don't like that man. I must get to know him better." To me, that is the very core of the Law of Polarity in relation to personal interactions.

Train your eyes to find the positive in every situation and person you encounter, and all the failures and frustrations in your life will be that much easier to bear. We all have a choice in how we see the "bad" things that happen to us. We can fixate on the negative and embrace the disappointment, or we can look for the positive that came with the negative. Often the positives that we identify won't undo the frustration in our minds, but any positive we can spot will make the disappointment a little easier to swallow.

The Law of Polarity assures us there is always a positive to find. If you don't see it yet, keep looking.

Quick Tip for Polarity: Have to deal with someone you cannot stand? Make it a game to find something about that person that you can appreciate or respect. Maybe you can appreciate his conviction or feel some compassion for her dealing with a rough situation. If nothing else, appreciate that you are not like this person before you and use this as a lesson to not become so.

The Law Of Cause And Effect

THINK OF LIFE as one big game of tumbling dominoes. For every event that happens, there was a precipitating cause that led to that event, the effect, which you are now experiencing. And every cause will create a specific effect. A person could write volumes about the implications and applications of the Law of Cause and Effect in the Universe. I am personally most familiar with the application of this Law as it relates to energy. Specifically, the understanding that the energy we put out into the Universe becomes the same energy we then attract to us.

When you put negative energy out with thoughts or actions, perhaps with a rude attitude or by demeaning or judging others, you are attracting that same negative energy back to you. When you emit feelings of hatred or jealousy, you will experience similar negative feelings directed your way.

When you go out into the world with love and gratitude, you are able to see that same positive energy attracted back to you, often in greater abundance.

The Law of Cause and Effect is at the heart of the Golden Rule, "Do unto others as you would have others do unto you." When you put out positive energy to your friends, they will put the same energy back to you. This may not be easy to see on the micro scale, as there will certainly be times when you are a complete grump with your friends, and they respond with care and understanding. There will also be times when you put positive energy and love into a relationship, but your friends respond with occasional anger and a bad attitude. There are many other factors at work in our day-to-day interactions with others, but on the larger scale, and over periods of time, if you regularly act in a kind, gentle and loving way toward those around you, you will find that people generally treat you in the same way.

Author and motivational speaker Zig Ziglar reminds us, "If you go out looking for friends, you're going to find they are very scarce. If you go out to be a friend, you'll find them everywhere."

Another implication of this Law, which is applicable in our daily interactions, is that if you respond to an angry or frustrated friend with an equally negative attitude, it will never make the situation better. Any experience with another person, whether it be a good or bad one, will always be made better with your positive contribution, just as the same experiences will always be made worse by your negative contribution.

Each of us has a specific energy vibration we are emitting all the time. Everyone around us can feel that energy. Most of the time, our energy is neutral or only slightly positive or negative. (Although, if I've done my job correctly, you should certainly maintain a positive energy vibration upon finishing this book!)

We, as humans, are sensitive to the energy being emitted by others, particularly when that energy is extreme.

When we pass someone on the street who is in the midst of a screaming argument with another person on the phone, we can feel the negative energy they are emitting. When we are in a store and a customer becomes irate with the cashier, we also pick up on that energy. On the other hand, when we are in a room with someone who is very positive and happy and who wears a big smile on his or her face, we can feel the positive energy they emit. This is what people mean when they talk about someone being "a ray of sunshine."

When someone expresses a positive gesture toward you, you automatically develop positive emotions in response. Conversely, when someone yells at you, you can feel your blood beginning to boil as a result of his or her angry energy.

If you raise your voice at a scared or upset child, they will only become more scared and upset. However, if you calmly talk in a soft and soothing voice to a child who is throwing a temper tantrum, they will respond by calming down much sooner. Unfortunately, it isn't always easy to catch ourselves in the moment and respond in this way.

I love to experiment with this Law because I enjoy the instant results it can bring. The next time you venture out into public, address people with an unusually positive and optimistic greeting. Show enthusiasm for being in their presence by acknowledging them. I like to greet people by saying, "Hello, how are you doing today?" Plenty of people ask similar questions, but then ramble on about needing a table for dinner or immediately turn their attention back to their cell phones. I don't do that. I smile and wait for a response.

Most of the time, this will catch the recipient off guard as they realize I am actually acknowledging them and care about their day. I challenge you to attempt the same. The reaction to this small gesture and the warmth you spread with your smile and compassion can be seen immediately on the faces of those you encounter. You will see the positive vibes strike them and affect the energy they feel. Your cause of positive energy creates a positive effect on their emotional state.

This application of the Law of Cause and Effect explains that the positive energy you send out into the world affects the energy balance of the world around you. When enthusiastic and positive, you cross paths with people, and they feel better for it. You bring sunshine into dark and cold rooms when you enter with a big smile and have happiness to share. Everyone in the room benefits as a result. Simply by emitting positive energy, you can become a creator of good; you possess the power to turn bad things into good. Knowing this possibility exists, why would you want to go through life any other way?

Quick Tip for Cause and Effect: The next time you find yourself in an environment surrounded by negative emotions and grumpy people, be an obnoxious and overwhelming source of positivity and optimism. During a family gathering where everyone seems grumpy and negative, or at the workplace when everyone feels stressed and anxious, emit a burst of positive energy through your actions and words, and it will create an effect in those around you. Your positive energy can be enough to plant a seed that changes the energy you attract back to you.

The Law Of Rhythm

THE LAW OF RHYTHM says that there is a natural ebb and flow to all things in life. Nothing is static; everything is constantly changing. That change does not continue in a straight progression. Instead, like a stock chart, even things that are on an upward trend can have periods of regression.

We experience this same rhythm in nature with the motion of the tides; water comes in for a while and then it goes back out. The sun comes up and the day gets brighter, then the sun goes down and night falls.

We also experience this Law playing out in our own lives; some days are simply better than others. Even during periods of drastic progression, we have setbacks. In the best of relationships, we have times that are rough. In the worst of life's challenges, we often get a few moments during the struggle to catch our breath—what is known by some as the eye of the storm.

This progression through better and worse times is rhythmic in nature and something we can plan for. A wonderful day or period in your life is certain to be followed by an experience that isn't as bright. When times are tough and you feel down and out, hang in there and try to remember that things will eventually improve.

Understanding the Law of Rhythm is important so that we don't fight this natural phenomenon. There is a purpose to the rhythm and a chance to capitalize on each phase. Hard experiences, when we are at our lowest, are required to prepare us for the next height of achievement. We only grow stronger when challenged or made uncomfortable.

The downswing motivates us to prepare and work for the next upswing. When we find ourselves at the next height of success, happiness or achievement, we get to appreciate it that much more because we know what it is like to be in the dumps. By reflecting on the hard times we have faced, we can appreciate their purpose much more when we recognize them as the natural rhythm that prepares us for the next high.

Just remember, when times are tough and you feel like the world is stacked against you, hang in there for a moment and trust that the tides will eventually shift. The worst days in our lives are followed by days that become progressively better. The darkest hour is just before the dawn.

Quick Tip for Rhythm: When times seem almost unbearable, think of a time in the days or weeks to come when things will be much better. If you are drained by the weekday routine, think of the time you will have to relax on the weekend. If you feel at your wits end while racing around to get work things done and the household in order before an upcoming business trip, imagine the calmness you will feel when you sink into the seat on the plane and all of the frantic hustle is behind you. Work through the task at hand, but remember your reprieve is just a few weeks, days or hours away.

The Law Of Gender

WHEN DISCUSSING THE LAW OF GENDER, we aren't talking about the differences between male and female. Instead, Gender in this context is derived from the old French word, gendrer, which is defined to mean the same as engender, beget, give birth to, or produce. In this sense, the Law of Gender suggests that all things take time to transpire. Much like gestation, when you plant a seed in the soil, it takes time for the plant to grow and the flower to bloom.

The same can be said of the goals and ambitions we pursue. The most precious ambitions take the greatest time to pass, but the goals we work to achieve will appear at the time and place they are supposed to.

In other words, everything that develops in our lives takes a certain amount of time to come to fruition. All dreams, goals and ambitions, like a seed planted in the soil, take a certain amount of time to gestate before you can harvest the fruit of your efforts.

I take comfort in this Law, as it reminds me that my next great achievement doesn't need to arrive at the end of this day or week. Sometimes, our most admirable goals take the longest to cultivate. When things get tough and it seems like nothing will ever change, remember that everything in life takes a certain amount of time to come to fruition.

Of course, this is an easier concept to appreciate in hindsight, especially for major developments in our lives that take some time to complete. Twenty years into a relationship with your best friend, you can appreciate all the time, energy and experiences that went into developing that relationship. When you graduate from high school or college, you can appreciate all the work that went into arriving at that goal. It is much harder to appreciate this Law when you are taking the first steps toward an enormous challenge. When stepping into the first class of freshmen year, the work that lies between you and graduation can be daunting.

Students of the Law of Attraction are taught to accept that their goals and desires will manifest at the precise time the Universe deems right. Theologians understand that God will bless us with the fruits of our devotion, again, only when the time is right.

Whether you understand this Law of Gender from a metaphysical or spiritual sense, each conclusion is the same.

If things aren't changing for you now, know in your heart and mind that they will eventually, as long as you continue to forge ahead. If the results you are seeking have not manifested in the time you thought was appropriate, this is a message to you that you must change your actions or continue to grow before you will experience the fruits of your labor.

Quick Tip for Gender: The next time you are in the midst of a pursuit that seems to have no end, stop for a moment to close your eyes and visualize the resulting goal you are striving for. When you are frustrated or upset by the seemingly lack of progress toward what you are working hard to achieve, imagine in detail what that achievement will feel like when it does come. Whether imagining graduation from college in a few years or the awesome success of your new business venture that won't be achieved for many years, use visualization to bring that great feeling of eventual manifestation to you today. Tap into that joy and excitement of finally achieving the big goal, and use that energy to push you through the grind you presently face.

The Law Of Transmutation Of Energy

ENERGY CANNOT BE CREATED or destroyed, it can only change form. This Law holds just as true for the energy of physical things, like your car, as it does for the emotional energy that we have stored within us.

If you sit on your bike at the top of a hill, you have a certain amount of potential energy that is due to your height atop that hill. When you kick off and begin to roll down the hill, that potential energy is transmuted into kinetic energy as gravity affects you and you pick up speed. Nearing the bottom of the hill, you will eventually lose speed as friction steals your energy by transmuting it into other forms of energy, like sound and heat. If you turn around and choose to ride back to the top of the hill, you will have to pedal your bike, expending energy you create with your muscles from the food you have consumed. That energy will allow you to transmute your physical kinetic energy (energy of motion) back into potential energy as you climb back up the hill.

The key point here is that the total amount of energy never changed; it was just transmuted from one form to another by various means.

I tend to be a very visual learner, so understanding how this Law works in the physical sense is helpful for me. But if that example just went completely over your head, don't worry—we can explore it on a different level.

This principle holds true with our emotional energy as well. The emotional energy we have must come from somewhere. When we think about something that either inspires us or frustrates us, we are creating that emotional energy we feel from the thoughts in our mind. Our thoughts are a means of changing the energy from the food we eat into emotional energy. Our emotional energy can then be transmuted back to physical energy when we are inspired to take action, either negative or positive.

Either way, there is always an exchange of energy going on.

When you are upset and you pound your fist against a punching bag, you release some of that negative emotional energy by transmuting it into the physical energy you are expending. The same is true for going out for a run after a negative interaction to blow off steam.

Positive emotional energy can also be transmuted through physical acts of love or kindness. These acts tend to share your positive emotional energy with the recipients, who then feel the boost from that energy.

Makes sense so far, right? But what if I told you that this transmutation of energy can also be used to transmute negative energy into positive? Or vice versa?

The power of our mind, and its ability to change negative to positive is truly fascinating. When we feel a negative emotion, we don't need to respond or create a negative action. Instead, if we are open to this transmutation, our negative emotions of disgust or frustration can inspire us to take positive actions that will create positive results. For instance, if someone who was bullied as a child grows up and creates an advocacy group for other victims of bullying which offers a safe harbor where all children can feel welcomed and accepted, they have transmuted the negative emotional energy from a traumatic childhood experience into a positive action that serves to help others.

Conversely, a person may feel a great deal of self-confidence, which is a positive emotion. But if they allow that self-confidence to drive actions of greed and selfishness, they have transmuted that positive energy into negative.

I wanted to discuss this Universal Law last because of the power I see in being able to convert negative energy into positive.

We may occasionally find ourselves in a position where we just can't shake a negative thought from our minds, even after considering an event in our lives through the context of Relativity, Polarity, Gender or Rhythm. It is in those cases that an understanding of the Law of Transmutation can allow us to at least convert that energy into something positive.

If we don't find a way to change this negative energy to positive, it will affect our vibration, and we will tend toward more negative energy and manifestations. Still, it isn't always so simple.

The premature death of a child or the loss of many in your community to a natural disaster are just two examples of any number of experiences that may be extremely difficult to see in a positive light, even when employing the Universal Laws. Through the Transmutation of Energy, however, you can embrace that pain and anger and use it to feed positive actions as a result.

Nick Vujicic is a motivational speaker who happens to have been born with no arms or legs. He could exhibit anger and frustration toward the Universe over the struggles he was born into, and no one would ever fault him for that. Fortunately for him and for the many lives he has changed through his motivational speaking and life coaching, Vujicic found a way to transmute potentially massive amounts of negative emotional energy into greater positive energy. As a result, he has inspired an incredible positive effect on the world around him.

Nick is certainly not the only person who has done this, though. We often hear of surviving spouses or parents of car accident victims that transmute their energy into positive action by taking on a life of advocacy. Parents of children who die of cancer commonly transmute their pain and anger into massive positive energy by committing their lives to raising awareness and money for cancer research. And children who at a young age lost a parent to illness have been known to grow up and enter medicine or research fields where they may be able to help others with the same disease.

When all else fails and you just can't see your circumstance in a positive light, harness that negative energy and transmute it into positive action.

Quick Tip for Transmutation of Energy: Anger and frustration can be awesome motivators. When you get worked up over something that must change, pour that energy into creating an action plan for change. The next time you feel disgusted by the number on the scale or your appearance in a bathing suit, scared by the balance of your checking account, or angered by the job you must walk into, use these emotions to effect drastic change. Don't ignore the feelings in hopes they will evaporate or distract your mind by thinking of something else; tap into the intense emotion and use it to drive your actions in a new and better direction.

Section One

———————— ◎ ————————

Bite-Size Recap

T HESE UNIVERSAL LAWS will provide the lens to find a sil-ver-lining in all life events. When you remind yourself that a movie is fictitious, you can prevent the emotional response you would otherwise experience. Empowered by the Universal Laws, you can remind yourself of the positive aspect of challenges and woes, thus helping you to hold a more positive outlook and energy in your life. We can then invest this enhanced positive vibration into the words and deeds we commit with our Action Sphere.

A firm understanding of the Universal Laws is important for properly managing your spheres. As you work through the rest of this book, you may find it beneficial to revisit this section to refresh your understanding of each Law and how they all can help you to find the positive in every event or circumstance you face in life.

To assist you in that endeavor, I will be wrapping up each of the four sections in this book with a quick recap you can return to at any time. For years, I have carried similar notes with me in a notebook or on my phone so I have them readily available during times of reflection. More than once, while in the midst of a particularly frustrating experience or challenging life event, my Universal Laws list has served as the reminder I need to find and understand the positive that may have otherwise been eluding me.

You will also find some suggested exercises at the end of each section to help you put the concepts you have learned to the test as you work to understand the real world implications of what we are discussing. I would encourage you to give these exercises a try. Not only can they greatly enhance your understanding of the concepts at hand, but they have also been specifically designed to help you harness the true power available to you when you begin to live your life with The Universal Laws in mind, keeping your sights focused on managing your Spheres.

- **Event:** Something that happened to you, like getting fired from your job.

- **Circumstance:** An aspect of your life or the world around you, like now being unemployed.

- **The Law of Vibration:** Like attracts like; you get back what you put out.

- **The Law of Relativity:** Nothing is either good or bad until you compare it to something else.

- **The Law of Polarity:** With every good comes an equal and opposite bad. And vice versa.

- **The Law of Cause and Effect:** Your actions have consequences, both good and bad. Every effect starts with a cause.

- **The Law of Rhythm:** Life resides in a constant state of change, full of peaks and valleys. Hard times can't endure forever, and the good should be cherished while it lasts.

- **The Law of Gender:** The seeds you plant today, both positive and negative, won't necessarily bear fruit tomorrow, but will always come to fruition at some point down the line.

- **The Law of Transmutation of Energy:** Physical and emotional energy cannot be destroyed but can change form.

When struggling with hard times in your life or looking for a way to change undesirable circumstances, work your way through these Laws to find the positive and shift your vibration. If all else fails, transmute that energy into something positive and powerful.

If you would like to find more resources about the Universal Laws, be sure to check out www.GarretBiss.com where you can download a Universal Laws quick reference guide or check out more information about the *A Life Unchained* series.

Section One

Applying What You've Learned

B EFORE MOVING ON, consider giving these exercises a try to help you commit the Laws to memory and see them working in your day-to-day life.

Write It Down

I AM A TRUE BELIEVER in the power of journaling. Putting words on paper helps to solidify ideas. Reflection on what you have written can reveal lessons you may not have learned in the moment. So I want you to take on a journaling exercise in order to see the power of the Laws in the management of your own vibration. Commit right now to two weeks of journaling every single day. You don't have to write a novel, but spending 10 minutes a day reflecting on the experiences of the day is one of the most respected tools for personal growth.

For this exercise, I want you to write with a slightly different focus for each of the next two weeks. I have your instructions for Week One here so you can begin as you continue reading the book.

I've included your instructions for Week Two at the end of this book, in the *Exercises Appendix*. Don't skip ahead and read it just yet. Get through Week One first and then flip to the back for your next set of instructions.

Week One: For this week, I want you to complete two tasks with your journaling:

Write a number at the start of each page, 1 through 10, to reflect how good or bad your day was.

Recall the main events that made your day a 1, a 10, or anything in between.

That's it. A number and a list of events contributing to that number. You can be as brief or in depth as you choose with that list—as long as what you are writing is something that will trigger the memories of what occurred for you when you look back.

> **Helpful Tip:** While I have personally experienced the power of writing words on paper in order to reflect back, I understand that writing is not everyone's forte. If the idea of sitting down and penning a journal every day sounds painful to you, and you consider yourself more of an audio learner, use your cell phone to create audio recordings of yourself vocally reflecting back every day. Just be sure to save each of those recordings to a separate file on your computer for listening to later.

Name That Law

LET'S PLAY A FUN GAME of "Name That Law!" I'm going to outline three different scenarios for you, each using fictional characters, and I want you to determine which Law is at play.

Note: You can find your answers in the Exercise Appendix at the back of this book.

Scenario One: Raphael is the first member of his family to attend college. Paying his tuition has not been easy, and in order to take as few student loans out as possible, he works twenty hours a week, on top of keeping up with a full course load. There are days when he is exhausted and plenty of times when he misses out on social activities the rest of his peers are enjoying. But Raphael always has a smile on his face, and whenever anyone asks him how he does it all, he reminds them that the pot of gold at the end of this rainbow is that degree he is working toward, which will not only help him get his dream job but will also make his family so proud.

What Law is Raphael using?

Scenario Two: Sandra was in a car accident on the way to work. She hit a patch of black ice, which caused her car to swerve into the vehicle driving the next lane over. Both cars were badly wrecked, but she and the other driver walked away with minimal injuries. Unfortunately, Sandra's insurance does not cover a rental vehicle while her car is being repaired, and she will also have to pay out a $500 deductible for those repairs—a lot of money for her at the time. She could be exceedingly frustrated and upset over this turn of events, but instead can't help but remember a similar accident she read about a year ago that proved fatal for one of the drivers. Rather than dwelling on the difficulties this accident now presents to her life, she is choosing to be thankful that both she and the other driver walked away relatively unharmed.

What Law is Sandra using?

Scenario Three: Chris and Emily met as teenagers at an Al-Anon group, for friends and family members of alcoholics. Both were in foster care as a result of a history of abuse at the hands of their alcoholic parents. Their foster care situations were not ideal, as they had each been moved between homes quite often. They both struggled with anger and feelings of depression over their circumstances and the tragic lives they had led up to this point. But through their friendship, as well as talking to other teenagers in similar situations, they began to build upon a shared passion for helping other children in foster care. They formed an advocacy group made up of current and former foster care youth in their area and began working toward reforms to improve the foster care experience, including playing a hand in increasing the age children could remain in foster care from 18 to 21. They spoke to legislative groups, raised awareness, and were integral in encouraging more families to provide loving homes for children in foster care. As adults, both Chris and Emily remain committed to making a difference for those still in foster care and to empowering other children facing similar struggles as they once did.

What Law are Chris and Emily using?

Bonus Challenge: Spend the next week actively looking for examples of the Laws at work in the world around you. Jot down every example you see, and reflect back on those examples at the end of the week.

Section Two:

Understanding and Managing Your Spheres

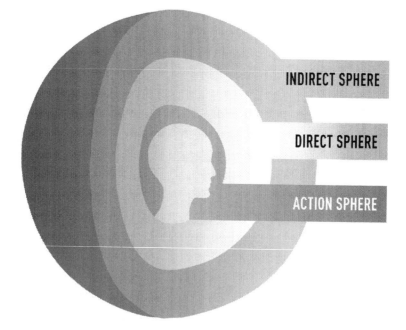

INDIRECT SPHERE

DIRECT SPHERE

ACTION SPHERE

Chapter 3

─────────── ◎ ───────────

The Spheres

L IFE IS ALL ABOUT PRIORITIES. Whether we want to admit it or not, none of us has the time or energy to devote to all of the things that we would like to. Even when life is going mostly as planned, we have to prioritize and accept that we can't have, do, and be everything at the same time. So when extraneous events steal the precious time that we were already working so hard to allocate responsibly, it can be devastating to our happiness. When you can find ways to regain that time and energy, you have more to invest in the things that *do* matter, thus achieving a happier and more enjoyable life experience.

That is where the "Spheres" I have been talking about come into play.

So, what are those Spheres and how does understanding them enable you to better manage your life for greater happiness, fulfillment and reduced stress?

If you will, picture the world around you as being comprised of three concentric spheres. You may envision these spheres as bubbles of different sizes that encompass you at the very center. We have already referenced these as the Indirect Sphere, the Direct Sphere and the Action Sphere.

The Indirect Sphere

T HE **INDIRECT SPHERE** is the largest, outermost Sphere. This Sphere is comprised of everything that happens in the world that is beyond our control and has no direct influence over us. Hence, the "Indirect" label. These are the events and circumstances that affect us indirectly, at best.

Consider the news of a celebrity divorce. Perhaps it is someone you like, a person whose movies you have always enjoyed or whose concerts you have attended. Maybe seeing pictures of them with their family has made you smile in the past. But this is not someone you personally know or interact with in any way. His or her divorce does not directly affect you.

That said, it does have the power to have an effect over you—if you allow it to. How invested you become in this news is completely up to you. If you spend hours poring over gossip magazines and searching for clues behind the celebrity splits, you are devoting valuable time and energy to an event that has nothing to do with you, diverting that time and energy from the things you can control.

An easy way to determine if something directly or indirectly affects us is by asking whether or not we *need* to respond to it. If a riot occurs a few thousand miles away, and you don't know anyone involved, there is nothing you *have* to do (physically or emotionally) to respond to that event.

If, on the other hand, the hot water heater in your house springs a leak, there is no way you can choose to not let that affect you. You *have* to do something in response.

Now, is it normal to have an emotional response to something tragic happening in the world, even if it doesn't directly affect you? Absolutely. And, in fact, there can be a lot of benefits from choosing to respond to certain events that speak to you emotionally, either through donating your time or funds. But the point is, you have a choice when it comes to how you respond to events and circumstances in the Indirect Sphere. You don't *have* to respond to any of it.

All past events also belong in the Indirect Sphere, as these events are no longer in your control. You may have a lingering circumstance from a past event that you can still affect (perhaps working to make amends to someone you have hurt), but you cannot change the past. No amount of fretting about your mistake or regretting an action will change the circumstance you now face, and lost energy and attention spent dwelling on that past event will only cost energy you could otherwise invest in changing your circumstances.

I have made mistakes in my past and done things I wish I hadn't. My relationship history is a perfect example of that. When my marriage hit rock bottom and I realized my wife and I were heading to a divorce, there were many memories from my past that would haunt my thoughts and divert my energy. I spent a significant amount of time dwelling over missed opportunities to connect or communicate: the evenings I worked late which, in hindsight, I didn't have to, the apologies I never gave, the compliments I failed to share and the arguments I should have avoided.

Each of these past events contributed to the future circumstance of me being single. During the course of our separation, I spent a lot of time reliving those past events in my mind and punishing myself for the choices I made and the things I could have done differently.

All that time spent living in the past was time and energy I couldn't spend doing anything about my present circumstances.

I was dwelling on the past instead of developing plans, skills, habits, or anything else that might help make my future better than my past.

There is always something to gain by reflecting on past events— the best way to grow for the future is to learn from our past. But there is a certain point where reflecting on the past goes from constructive to destructive and from a tool we can use for a better tomorrow to a negative thief of our positive energy.

The past is just one example; if you allow something negative in your Indirect Sphere to occupy your mind, it will inevitably take a toll on your emotions, and ultimately your activity. Dwelling on these Indirect Sphere events pulls your attention from the aspects of your life that should otherwise matter most.

There are, of course, many good things that occur in our Indirect Sphere. Hearing a story of a heroic event that saved lives or an everyday story about a stranger committing a kind act to help another, can motivate us to be better versions of ourselves. Maybe you've read an inspiring book about someone overcoming tough odds to achieve their dreams or helping to make the dreams of others come true. These stories are Indirect Sphere events that can bring positive emotions to your life.

If we choose to be touched by these Indirect Sphere events and circumstances in a positive way, we can actually gain quite a bit: inspiration, motivation, compassion, and a slew of other positive emotions. As long as the time we spend thinking about those events and circumstances doesn't distract us from dealing with the things we must respond to or can control, there is plenty to be learned by reflecting on Indirect Sphere occurrences or the experiences of others.

The important thing to understand about the Indirect Sphere is that the events here *can* affect us if we allow them to. If we let the news of tragedies occurring a thousand miles away fester in our minds or occupy our attention, this will have an effect on our emotions and our actions as a result. If we spend too much time dwelling on Indirect Sphere events, it consumes our time to deal with the things that we must respond to and can affect.

I am not suggesting that we ignore the Indirect Sphere or pretend it doesn't exist. Rather, be aware that many things in the world don't really have to affect us if we choose not to let them.

The Direct Sphere

T HE **DIRECT SPHERE** is comprised of all the events and circumstances in life that directly affect us—the ones that force us to respond or react in some way. Events in this Sphere may include losing your wallet, the bad weather that occurs on your day off, or the harsh words your boss spoke to you. Each of the events or circumstances within the Direct Sphere elicits some form of reaction.

Let's say your distant neighbor loses his job. You can recognize this as a terrible and unfortunate event, but it is not one that directly affects you or your family. It is an Indirect Sphere event. You may respond, but you don't have to.

If *you* lose your job, on the other hand, that would be a Direct Sphere event. You have to respond in some way; if you don't, you and your family will soon go hungry and wind up on the streets. Still, how you respond is up to you. You have a choice whether this Direct Sphere event will spark a downward spiral of emotional turmoil or elicit constructive action on your part.

With Indirect Sphere events, you choose *whether* you react or respond. With Direct Sphere events, you choose *how you* will react or respond.

Both Indirect and Direct Sphere events and circumstances can be seen in a positive or negative light. The Universal Laws empower you to find the positive side of every event that occurs.

Once an event is brought to your attention, filter that event in your mind to decipher whether it directly affects you or not. Then, discard Indirect Sphere events from your thoughts and turn your focus back to the Direct Sphere items on your plate.

The Action Sphere

T HE LAST SPHERE is the **Action Sphere.** This Sphere encompasses everything in the world we can affect ourselves. The Action Sphere can extend both directly and indirectly beyond you to all the people and things you control or influence with your actions and words.

Let's say you decide to volunteer for Big Brothers Big Sisters. You take a "Little" under your wings and commit to spending time with him or her once a week. You introduce your Little to experiences they never would have had otherwise and provide encouragement and sound advice they aren't getting at home. As a result of your guidance and mentorship, your Little blossoms in school and decides to pursue a college degree. Ultimately, he or she rises above the circumstances of his or her home life and goes on to live a productive and happy existence—possibly becoming a Big Brother or Sister themselves a decade or two down the line.

That is an example of your Action Sphere at work.

The actions we take today have an influence on the world we experience tomorrow. The events we create this year help to define the circumstances we see in the next. The Action Sphere extends as far as your voice and actions can travel, which today, with the Internet, blogs and social media, can reach pretty far. The Action Sphere also extends outward, to all that you can affect with your personal actions—the people you help, the work you do and the legacy you build with your own hands. When your actions inspire the actions of another, then your Action Sphere extends indirectly through all they can reach as well.

It's Not All About Size

I've DESCRIBED THE SPHERES in order of size, simply because that is the easiest way to picture them. But just to clarify—these Spheres can't be physically defined. And even if they could be, they would be in constant flux.

The boundaries between the Direct and Indirect Sphere are determined based on how events and circumstances affect us. It isn't about how far that sphere reaches, but rather about the effect the events and circumstances within that sphere have over you. Something may happen to a friend 500 miles away that absolutely affects you. And at the same time, a neighbor down the street could be going through something that doesn't affect you at all.

The visual metaphor of three Spheres, with the Indirect Sphere being the largest, just illustrates that there are many more events and circumstances going on in the world that don't directly affect you than those that do.

When you are first introduced to this concept of Spheres, there are likely to be many Indirect events and circumstance that presently reside in your Direct Sphere. This simply means there are things occurring around you that are having a direct impact on your emotions or happiness, even though they shouldn't. If a tragedy on the news or a memory of the past has held a string to your emotions, you are allowing these events to operate like Direct Sphere events.

With awareness, you can move events and circumstances that shouldn't affect you directly to where they belong, the Indirect Sphere.

You shrink the Direct Sphere by not committing energy to worrying about events and circumstances that don't directly affect you. If the wins and losses of your favorite sports team dictate the mood you carry and the energy you emit in the days following a game, this would be an example of something you are allowing to reside in your Direct Sphere that doesn't need to. Similarly, if the fictitious life events of a character on your favorite TV show affect your emotional vibration for a day or two, you are allowing that show to have a direct effect on you and possibly the actions you take.

When you let these things slip into your Direct Sphere, the sphere grows because there are now more things in the world permitted to affect your thoughts, emotions and actions. In these examples, your Direct Sphere is artificially inflated because of the Indirect Sphere intruders you have allowed in.

When you "shrink" your Direct Sphere, you are merely identifying the indirect intruders and pushing them back to the Indirect Sphere where they belong. The ideal goal would be to shrink your Direct Sphere as small as you can, greatly reducing the events and circumstances that hold a direct connection to your thoughts, emotions, actions and ultimately the results and blessings you receive into your life.

The Action Sphere can be harder to visualize in this regard. I introduced the Action Sphere conceptually as the smallest of the three, but it has the ability to reach beyond anything you might now imagine. The size of this Sphere has everything to do with the influence you have on the world around you, and the ripples you create through your actions. The more you increase your own reach, the larger your Action Sphere will become.

I like to imagine them as three concentric Spheres with me in the middle, but this is just where the analogy begins.

The Road Trip

ONE MAJOR GOAL of this book is to help you identify the things that lay in the Indirect Sphere, those things that are beyond your control and direct influence so that you can clear them from your concern. Once you do this, you can reinvest that saved time and energy in dealing with the things you must concern yourself with—the events within the realm of the Direct Sphere. From there, you will be able to make the most of your Action Sphere.

As a visual person myself, I love describing ideas in analogies I can picture in my mind. Let's try an analogy that may help you understand and decipher these three Spheres.

Imagine you have just finished a wonderful vacation with your family at Disney World. It was a great trip, but you aren't especially looking forward to the 1,200-mile drive home you now face. You have your route mapped out and know what roads you will bet traveling, as you have done this drive before. Picture the entire interstate system in America as being representative of the largest Sphere, your Indirect Sphere.

Things in the Indirect Sphere can affect us, but only if we choose to let them. Let's imagine that it happens to be Memorial Day weekend. On the news and radio, there will certainly be stories about the record number of motorists taking to the road. It is the start of summer, so there are also stories about rising gas prices. National traffic accident rates are increasing, and serious traffic congestion has been reported in nearly every major city. These stories continue to broadcast on the radio as you start out on your drive.

It makes sense that all of this negative news might affect you. At the start of a long road trip, with various reports about terrible traffic across the country, most people would likely feel a little anxious to get this stupid drive over with. Maybe all you can picture is sitting in bumper to bumper traffic, shelling out hundreds of dollars more on fuel than you care to spend, and driving late into the night while exhausted, just to make up for time delays from the extra traffic.

Each of these travel circumstances is only occurring in the Indirect Sphere so far, though. You have simply heard of them, and you haven't heard anything specifically pertaining to the roads you are traveling.

Yet, the traffic conditions *are* affecting you, at least indirectly, because of the emotional response they have created in your mind. It is a reaction you have permitted, not a situation that requires any kind of direct response from you. Just because there are expected travel delays across the country and fuel prices are up as a national average, it does not mean these things will be true for the course you take on *your* road trip. If you have allowed yourself to be affected already, it is only because you made the assumption that these things would actually happen to you as well.

High fuel prices in Arizona and Chicago have no relevance on a trip from Orlando to New York. A traffic jam on a road that runs westbound from Florida to California has no effect on those traveling north.

Even though we intuitively know this, we may still allow the knowledge of events that don't *actually* affect us to take a toll on our attitude and internal peace. If we dwell on the things reported in the news, we certainly won't be as happy as we could be. When distracted by these frustrations, we have a harder time enjoying our current situation. It becomes more difficult to focus on the beauty of the drive or enjoy a conversation with our kids.

It isn't just those news reports about traffic conditions that reside in the Indirect Sphere in this scenario, though. The plant you forgot to water before you left home is another perfect example. It isn't something that is touching you right now, and there is nothing you can do about it, so the only way it affects you is if you let it.

When we let these Indirect Sphere things enter our consciousness and occupy our mind, they steal our time and energy from Direct and Action Sphere priorities that we *can* actually affect. These Indirect Sphere events cloud our ability to enjoy life as we live it and to feel happiness in what we are doing in the moment.

This is when it might behoove you to turn off the radio, stop listening to the reports of traffic jams across the nation, and instead focus on enjoying the drive you are currently on.

This brings us to the Direct Sphere. What *does* directly affect us in this little analogy? What events and circumstances actually require a response?

The Direct Sphere is just the road you are on and the road slightly ahead of you. Of the entire interstate system, only a small stretch of road really matters to you at any given time–the stretch of road that will require you to react or respond in some way. You may have to slow down, speed up, change lanes, turn, detour, etc., but all of that is determined by what is occurring immediately around you.

Many things can enter this Direct Sphere that require your response. Let's imagine that you round a bend in the road and notice traffic has come to a standstill. Your navigation system identifies an accident just ahead. You see no sign that traffic will begin moving again anytime soon, and there are no exits you can take in search of a detour. It is already six at night, and you've been driving all day.

Your plan was to get home, unpack the car and get the kids in bed early. You wanted a good night's rest before returning to work in the morning. Now, it doesn't look like that is going to happen. But what can you do?

While we don't often control the events and circumstance that occur within the Direct Sphere, we do control how we respond to them. An event like a traffic jam is going to affect you; it is direct and can't be avoided. But your response is within your control. And how you respond will significantly affect your circumstances moving forward from this event.

So, what options might you have for responding? You could get angry and begin hitting the steering wheel in frustration. You could throw out a few curse words and scare your kids. You could also begin frantically looking for new routes, taking the last several hundred miles on side roads that would have you getting home closer to midnight.

Or, you could protect your vibration and search for something positive. The Law of Relativity suggests, relatively speaking, you are in a far better position than those involved in the accident ahead. You just had a great weekend with your family, and you have a job and house awaiting your return. Everyone in your car is healthy and safe. Maybe you could use this event as an opportunity to pull off the road and have a nice meal.

Sure, it isn't ideal, but your reaction is completely within your control. There are many tools we can use to help guide our thoughts and actions when challenges are presented.

As a bystander to this scenario, it is easy to understand that losing your cool, yelling and screaming, or feeding the frustration isn't going to make things better for anyone. Alternatively, finding some positive aspects presented by this event will make the rest of the day and road trip more enjoyable and upbeat for your own emotions and for everyone else. One response will ensure a decent evening; the other will lead to a disaster. The good news is, we have nearly unlimited control of the way we respond.

The choices we make not only affect our circumstances; they influence the circumstances of others as well. This is where the Action Sphere comes in. These are the events and circumstances that you can directly affect and you currently have control over. Your *reaction* to a Direct Sphere event extends into your Action Sphere.

What represents this Sphere in our road trip analogy? Remember, the Action Sphere is just what you can affect, namely your personal actions and the words you communicate.

You cannot control the vehicles around you, but you can control your own. You cannot control the behavior and mood of other motorists, the traffic on the road or the weather outside. No matter how much you may like to believe you can, you don't have full control over the attitudes and actions of the kids in the back seat or the passenger beside you. And you can't control the fact that the accident ahead has caused traffic to back up the way it has.

You can control your responses and actions. You get to choose when you stop for breaks and when you forge ahead. You have control over how Direct and Indirect Sphere events affect you emotionally. You certainly have control over the words that you say and the actions you take toward others around you.

In our example, the bubble of the whole world around us is the interstate system from coast to coast. Within those 3.8 million square miles of real estate, the only area you have direct control over is the bubble or Sphere of your vehicle and the thoughts within your head, which manifest your actions and mood. While that may seem insignificant, by the end of our discussion you will understand that the magnitude of what you can actually control is not as trivial as it may seem at first glance.

The 3 Spheres

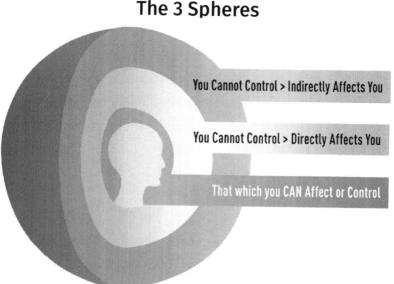

You Cannot Control > Indirectly Affects You

You Cannot Control > Directly Affects You

That which you CAN Affect or Control

Chapter 4

○

Sphere Management

V ERY FEW OF US would describe ourselves as negative people. But if you've ever felt stressed, disappointed, judgmental, victimized, helpless, angry, or irate... then you have harbored negative emotions. If you have gotten a result from life that you didn't want, or your current circumstances with work, finances, relationships, or your health are not what you would like, you have likely created (or at least aided) these manifestations in your life through your negative thoughts and vibration.

Many of us can feel this negative emotional or vibrational state for so long that it becomes our new norm—our new set point. I have been there myself. I have experienced times in my life where I was grumpy or depressed for so long that I didn't even recognize how innate those feelings had become. Negative vibration was the new me. I am not saying that during this period I never got happy or felt positive, but it was almost like I had moved my emotional origin from 0 (perfectly between positive and negative) down to a negative two or three. Every day I started out in a funk, and it took work or good fortune to move me to the positive.

If you haven't experienced this yourself, you may have seen it in friends or coworkers. Have you ever known someone who was always a grump, but was oblivious to it? Maybe they even had a smile on their face while they were complaining about things or spreading judgment about others. These people have a negative set point for their emotional vibration.

You yourself may be experiencing this and not even realize it. As humans, we are programmed to grow used to our circumstances—to the point that we don't even necessarily realize how bad those circumstances have become until something changes.

Let me give you a personal example. A few years ago, I decided to clean up my diet. I wanted to eat less processed food, add more vegetables, and begin drinking a lot more water.

After just a few weeks of this change, I couldn't believe how amazing I felt. I was sleeping better, experiencing better mental clarity, was more alert throughout the day, and had far more energy.

Before the diet change, I hadn't realized I was feeling as bad as I was because I had been that way for so long. The same can be true for your emotional vibration. After applying some of the suggestions shared in this book, you will find yourself in an overall better emotional state. If you were experiencing a prolonged, unnoticed funk, embracing the Universal Laws and managing your Spheres will help you to get your emotional set point back to zero and then beyond. If you were always an emotionally balanced, normally positive person, managing your Spheres will help you move your set point further in the positive direction... maybe so much so that you, too, can be one of those annoying people who are always happy, high on life, and experiencing everything manifesting just the way you desire. Oh, I used to hate those people... then I became one of them. Hey, if you can't beat them, join them!

Your thoughts are directly related to your results. Another, more insightful way to think of this—the results you've experienced are directly related to the thoughts which preceded them. Fortunately, you *can* control your thoughts; therefore, you can directly control the results you experience in life.

Understanding the differences between the Spheres is really just the first step. The real benefits come when you start managing your Spheres and, in turn, your life.

For enhanced understanding, I want to start by discussing the management of each Sphere in isolation. Of course, life doesn't just occur in one Sphere at a time. So, once we have the basics down, we will put everything together to show how these concepts can be applied in real life situations—situations where every Sphere may be affected at once.

But for now, let's work on managing one Sphere at a time.

Controlling Your Indirect Sphere

UNDERSTANDING AND PROPERLY managing the Indirect Sphere is the area that may make the greatest difference in your life. Remember, the Indirect Sphere is the Sphere of events and circumstances you can't control and that don't directly affect you. The only thing you can control in relation to this Sphere is how much emotional energy you devote to it.

When we can regain our energy and attention from the Indirect Sphere things that are stealing our time, we can redistribute that energy to the things that we can control. And we can use that time we gain to work more productively to find the positive from the Direct Sphere events and circumstances we are faced with.

Ultimately, we are all better off if we remember that our energy is best spent focused on the events and circumstances we can affect. This doesn't mean we cease to have compassion or care for those in circumstances that are occurring outside our personal realm of control, but it does mean that we are reasonable about how much energy we devote to the circumstances we cannot change. This is particularly true when those circumstances have no direct effect on us, as is the case with all events within the Indirect Sphere.

Motivational speaker and business philosopher Jim Rohn calls these things his "blame list"—everything in the world that might have been holding him down or preventing any greater success in his life.

As he tells it, he spent much of his youth looking for all the reasons beyond his control that contributed to his lack of prosperity and good fortune. Rohn, like so many of us, took comfort in his blame list because it served as a great excuse for why he didn't have more happiness, abundance and success. Made up completely of Indirect Sphere items, he had no control over anything on the blame list, so he could blame those items anytime to validate his lack of success.

Rohn recounts, "It was hard to give up the blame list. It was so comfortable blaming the government, negative relatives, a company policy, unions, wage scales, economy, interest rates, crisis and circumstances."

While there may be some circumstances in which these things do directly affect you and must be responded to (the union you are a part of declaring a strike, for instance) for most people, these are Indirect Sphere events and circumstances occurring outside your possible control or influence. Most of these things are news items you hear about but don't need to respond to directly.

Remember to use that as your point of reference when determining whether an event or circumstance belongs in the Indirect or Direct Sphere—the question of whether or not you need to respond or react to that event or circumstance in some way.

We may all worry about the things that were on Rohn's blame list, but we cannot directly affect them, and they don't directly affect us. Any indirect impact they have is only because we allow them that power. If we let them occupy our minds and influence our emotions and attitude, they will then affect our actions, which will in turn affect our results and future outcomes.

You may find that the best way to preserve your emotional energy when dealing with these events is to tune them out. Turn off the news if it affects you too deeply. Avoid political conversations with people who hold opposing views if they tend to get you riled up. And choose to shift your focus toward the events and circumstances that you can control and that stand to have the greatest positive impact on your life.

The Past

The Indirect Sphere also contains everything that has happened in our past, events that no longer hold any direct bearing over our lives today.

We all have regrets and hurts we are holding onto from the past. The love we let get away. The dream job we said "no" to. The personal feud we got into with a friend or loved one, and then didn't have a chance to resolve before that person passed away. The words we said that can never be taken back...

While it is true that things that have happened or decisions we have made in the past have created the life we are currently experiencing, there isn't anything we can do to change that past now. We may take actions and do things that alleviate a pain or challenge created by past events, but we cannot undo the past to make that challenge go away.

Think about it. You can work to pay off your credit card debt, but you can't change the fact that you racked it up in the first place.

Remember, the events that make up the Indirect Sphere are all things we cannot change, and obviously the past is something we can no longer alter. So, how do you keep it from cycling like a hamster on a wheel through your mind today?

Perhaps you made a mistake 10 years ago that changed the course of your life forever. Or maybe someone you deeply cared about hurt you in a way that made it difficult for you to trust anyone again. A lot of us are guilty of allowing our past to shape our future and of hanging onto events and circumstances that we likely should have let go of many years ago.

I want you to ask yourself what you actually gain by holding onto the past. It is important to learn lessons from our experiences and to apply those lessons to our future interactions and dealings with others, but obsessing about past events can deprive you of energy that would be better spent on cultivating the future you actually want. At some point, we should all find a way to accept the past for what it is and realize that we cannot change the circumstances that have already occurred. All we can do is learn from those experiences and move forward.

So, if you are holding onto the past, I would urge you to ask yourself why? For what purpose? Does any potential regret or remorse serve you in any positive way right now? When you realize you aren't served by holding onto that past, you find ways to let go of it and move forward.

This doesn't mean you should allow toxic people back into your life or plunge yourself right back into old and precarious situations. Rather, it means forgiving yourself for any missteps you may have made and allowing yourself to bury those past experiences so that you can create a clean slate for yourself to build upon now.

Whenever you find yourself obsessing over events from the past, remember that they can't be changed and that they, therefore, aren't worthy of your time and energy. The more focused you are on the past, the less you have to give to your present and future.

Sometimes, letting go of the past can feel impossible, though, and acknowledging that is okay. "Letting go" is not the only way to deal properly with Indirect Sphere items. I only suggest that first because anytime you can let it go, it is the easiest solution to embrace. Doing so will certainly save you the most time and frustration in dealing with these events. If you can will the dark clouds from the Indirect Sphere to vanish, you can more quickly refocus your attention on your Action Sphere and creating the life you desire.

But there are plenty of times we cannot just let things go. I know that, and have faced the same reality myself. When I personally find myself clinging to the past, I apply the Universal Laws to find whatever positive I can. If you can't push the dark cloud from your sky by letting it go, use the Universal Laws to at least transform that dark cloud into a nice puffy white one.

Remember that negativity from the Indirect Sphere influences your mood, creates fear, diminishes performance, and causes stress, which can impact your health and the actions you take today, darkening your outlook on life. Make a choice.

Managing Your Direct Sphere

H OW DO WE EASILY DETERMINE where the Indirect Sphere ends and the Direct Sphere begins?

The truth is, the ability to pinpoint the Sphere you are dealing in will come only with experience and may depend on a variety of details. Both the Indirect and Direct Spheres contain events and circumstances we cannot control. While we've discussed evaluating whether or not you are being directly affected (whether you need to respond or react), it is sometimes more complicated than a quick determination might allow.

For instance, while a housing market crash is typically an Indirect Sphere event, how does it change if you are currently in the position of needing to move for a job, and the value of your own home has just dropped by $100,000 due to the crash?

Let's say you've already asked the two main determining questions we've discussed:

Is the market crash event happening directly to me?
In our example, it's not exactly happening directly *to* you, but it is directly affecting you.

Is there some effect of the event that I must respond to, or could I simply side-step the event entirely and allow it to pass by?
You at least have a decision to make in this situation—do you move forward with trying to sell the house, knowing you will now lose money in doing so? Do you attempt to secure a loan modification or negotiate a short sale with the bank? Do you default on your mortgage and face the

consequences to your credit and ability to buy again? Or, do you explore other options, like renting the house until the housing market recovers, or declining the job offer and remaining where you are until a better time to sell? Simply sidestepping the event isn't really possible, as even inaction is a decision in a case like this.

The next thing to ask might be:

If I closed my eyes or refocused my mind, would this event still feel like a big deal in my life?

Closing your eyes and refocusing likely won't make this event go away—you still have big decisions to make as a result of this crash.

Occasionally, there may be a little disparity, so there is one more question that that might provide you clarity:

Is there anything I can do about this event or circumstance?

There is nothing you can do about the crash itself, but you can decide how to respond to the crash—thus altering the effect this event has on your life.

If you realize there is nothing you can do, that is typically a sign that you are dealing with an Indirect Sphere issue. But in this case, the answer is more complicated than that—moving this event into the Direct Sphere, mostly because while you can't alter the circumstances of the crash itself, you can make decisions that will determine how deeply that crash affects your life, given your own current personal circumstances.

The reason we must know the difference between the Direct and Indirect Spheres is that we must learn how to focus our energy on only the things that directly affect us, preserving our energy for the events and circumstances we have the power to affect ourselves. If you weren't in the position of needing to move, a housing crash would be an Indirect Sphere event you would be best served not worrying about.

Because you can't really manage your Direct Sphere without first gaining control of your Indirect Sphere, I want to take a moment to further highlight how these two Spheres can overlap.

Let's say news of the bad economy affects your mood. The country's fate weighs so heavily on your mind that you think all day about the possibility of losing your job. You take this attitude to work, and your preoccupation with the economy makes it hard for you to focus. You have a bad attitude toward others because you are living in fear. You lose the ability to perform as you once did and your productivity declines. You soon begin to feel subconsciously that your job isn't as fulfilling as it once was because you haven't enjoyed the work you have been doing there for the last few weeks. Now your emotions are on a downward spiral.

After a few weeks of dragging yourself out of bed to get to a job you don't want but are fearful of losing, all parts of your life are now affected. You are not as happy with friends and your negative feelings seep into your recreational time. You have lost balance in your life, so you are frustrated more easily and find less enjoyment than you once did in just about everything.

You have let something from the Indirect Sphere take hold of you and directly affect you. Unless you are on the board at your company, you likely have no control over whether or not there will be job cutbacks. You certainly cannot directly control whether or not the company will continue on a negative slide with employment. The only thing you do have some control over is whether or not you will lose your job. And the action of worrying about it won't do anything to protect that job.

What you can control is your attitude on the job. You can control your performance and the contribution you make toward the company that employs you. If you recognize that the economy is not something that directly affects you, you can make the simple choice to not allow it to indirectly affect you, either.

Understanding how to manage the Direct Sphere starts with recognizing what we can and cannot control. One way to think of the Direct Sphere is to see it as everything that is within arm's reach. These are the things that you push and pull at all day long, those that have a direct affect upon you. As with the Indirect Sphere, you lack control over what happens within the Direct Sphere. But unlike the Indirect Sphere, you can't simply ignore the events that occur within your Direct Sphere. They are happening to you, and you therefore must respond. But it is always up to you how you respond.

A perfect example might be a bad driver who keeps cutting you off on the way to work. Because this person is creating unsafe driving conditions, while also taking the same stretch of road you need to travel, you are being directly affected by a circumstance you can't directly control but must, in some way, respond to. Your options are to grow angry and begin driving aggressively in return or to pull back and allow this vehicle to get far enough ahead of you that they can no longer affect your driving experience. You could also continue driving at a safe distance while consciously monitoring this vehicle so that you can be prepared if they cut you off again.

Many people would get angry. We all feel possessive over our right of way on the road, after all, and unsafe drivers can easily frustrate us. But growing angry and responding by driving aggressively yourself only further perpetuates the unsafe driving conditions for all those around you. It isn't likely going to change this poor driver's behavior, and may actually only further aggravate whatever part of them is fueling this bad driving to begin with. At the very least, reacting with aggression on your part will increase your blood pressure and may lead to a ticket, or worse--an accident, thus making a bad situation worse—that downward spiral.

Instead, if you choose to take a deep breath and pull back, or to focus on your own safe driving in response, you not only do your part to provide for the safety of others on the road, you also create an environment where you aren't allowing this stranger to affect your mood or attitude any more than absolutely necessary.

A significant point to realize is that you have the ability to choose how everything in this Sphere affects you. And applying an understanding of the Universal Laws can help you to control that. If you want to allow a negative encounter at the morning meeting to ruin the rest of your day, you can do that. But if you would prefer to think of the situation in the context of Polarity or Relativity, and conclude that it really isn't a big deal in the grand scheme of things, you can do that as well.

Managing your Direct Sphere is all about protecting your vibration. Doing so inspires you to commit positive actions, which empowers the Law of Cause and Effect to work for you instead of against you. It is the difference between allowing one negative event to cloud your thoughts and emotions (thereby attracting more negativity) and searching for the positive so that you can move forward (thus producing your own positive effect).

Taking ownership of this can be difficult for people at first. Let's be honest; it is humbling to admit we have allowed some of the negative circumstances in our life to exist. The sooner you realize that your realm of control resides in how you react and respond to Direct Sphere events, the sooner you begin shrinking the level of negative influence this Sphere has over your life.

Using Your Action Sphere

THE ACTION SPHERE IS…where the action is! This Sphere consists of the time and space you have control over. With a little consideration about how actions and events inspire other actions and events, that control you hold is much farther reaching than you might first suspect.

We have all been in tough situations before; those circumstances where we felt out of control and at a loss for how to make things better. Perhaps you lost a job, leaving you feeling powerless and unable to find a solution for the money issues you knew were just around the corner. Or maybe you went through a bad breakup and are sure that you will never love or trust again.

It is in these times of despair when it may seem as though our Action Sphere has disappeared. You feel helpless and overwhelmed, so of course you assume that you truly have lost all control. On the contrary, though, there are always powerful tools we have at our disposal that can add a little sunshine to a terrible situation. Use what tools you *do* have to improve your positive vibration.

The ultimate purpose of managing our Action Sphere is to create positive vibrational energy within us, and to spread this positive energy to the people and environment surrounding us. Positive thoughts and emotions dispel the stress, anxiety, frustration, lack of confidence and helplessness that prevent us from living life as we want to. With these negative thoughts and emotions looming in our mind, we find our life to be less enjoyable and less fulfilling than it should. Managing our Action Sphere begins with our thoughts because these thoughts breed emotions and images in our mind which then dictate the actions we take and the results that we get from our life experience.

Two great tools you should always have ready in your Spheres Managing arsenal are the tool of gratitude and the tool of charity. The first develops positive energy within; the second helps spread that positive energy far beyond.

The Power Of Gratitude

G RATITUDE WAS FIRST MENTIONED as a Quick Tip in the Universal Laws discussion of vibration. By its nature, gratitude is a positive emotion that is spurred by positive thoughts. Because a positive thought and negative thought cannot coexist in our mind, thoughts of gratitude can be used to replace negative, self-defeating thoughts when they arise.

If you have ever tried to think of nothing at all, you know how impossible a task this can be, especially when trying to stop thinking about worries and concerns. The more effective approach is to replace negative thoughts with positive ones—in comes gratitude!

The next time you find yourself in a funk, stop and think of what you have to be grateful for, no matter how simple those things might be: the roof over your head, the food in your stomach, the air in your lungs and the blood in your veins. Be grateful for the things you don't have as well: things like a terminal illness, a broken bone or a black eye. If these new emotions don't completely change your situation, they will at least lend reprieve from the angst or frustration on your mind.

Thinking of the things you are grateful for stimulates a little positive emotional energy, but if you want to get the greatest benefit, write them down or say them aloud. The additional effort to hear, see and say the things you are grateful for makes the exercise significantly more effective.

Charity And Selflessness

SELFLESS AND CHARITABLE ACTS for the benefit of others can be the fastest way to improve the environment around you and to garner more enjoyment and fulfillment from the experience of life. I believe that many of the personal and societal ills we face as humanity can be traced back to thoughts of selfishness. And the quickest way to move beyond the issues of stress, anxiety or oppression and hatred is through selfless thoughts and actions.

If you question this idea, then consider how much positive energy is created from a kind or generous action you commit. Not only can you create a positive feeling in another through a selfless act, but it makes you feel better, too! Because of this, selfless or charitable acts can also be used as a tool to create a positive vibration within you, or to amplify your good emotions when you are already in a good emotional place.

Giving of ourselves for the benefit of others is often the purest form of gratitude. When you give your time, energy or money to another person, you are demonstrating to the Universe appreciation for what you already have. This action, through cause and effect, opens the floodgates for you to receive more and more to be grateful for.

Remember, the more you appreciate all that you have, the more the Universe wants to give!

I share some other examples and ideas about selfless acts, giving to charity, and the rewards we get in return in my book, *Charity The Gifts of Giving.*

Relying On The Laws

M ANY TIMES, WHEN WE FEEL overloaded with pressure or preoccupation of mind, we cut off the flow of positive energy that normally emanates from us. We "go internal" and focus our time and energy on thoughts and mental preparation. We guard our mind from distraction by focusing our attention inward, or on the task at hand. If you have ever been around someone going through an experience like this, they may seem cut off, fidgety and easily agitated.

Consider what the Law of Cause and Effect would say about this type of action and behavior. When we stop putting our normal positive energy out into the environment around us, how does that affect the way the Universe responds to us?

At a time when we need a surplus of good will from the Universe, we may be taking actions that are creating a deficit.

The next time you have such an event looming over you, try to take the opposite approach. Take purposeful actions to create a debt of positive energy from the Universe. Invest the energy you do have into being extra kind to others; buy something small for a friend or give money to charity. Give someone at work a compliment or help with a project they are working on.

There are many benefits you can gain from this change of philosophy and from the new actions you will take because of it. The Law of Cause and Effect says you will attract the same positive energy back to you—at a time when you really want it! Transmutation of energy will allow you to transform the nervous, and possibly negative, energy into something positive, which in turn raises your vibrational energy. The actions you are taking in your Sphere of Action will now make a difference in the environment of your Direct Sphere. By making the most of what you have to work with—your thoughts, words and actions—you can make the most of the effects you get from the Direct and Indirect Spheres.

Let's say some big event in your life doesn't go the way you had hoped it would. You worked to increase your positive energy, and things still didn't work out in your favor. Maybe the sale you wanted to make didn't happen, or you didn't get the A you needed on your exam. Still, because you took actions that helped put you into such a positive state to begin with, instead of allowing your energy to slowly dissipate by "going internal," you are now in a good vibrational state, and you will be able to handle the failure better than you otherwise would have. The confidence you will have while in this positive state will allow you to remember the Universal Laws and find the positive that mitigates the negative feeling from the loss or failure.

When you are in a positive state, it is easier to see the positive around you. When we are in a negative state, the most prevalent thoughts and facts we tend to attract to our attention are other negatives.

These effects from the actions we take extend so far beyond just ourselves. These days, we can reach literally around the world in a matter of seconds. The words we share on the Internet live forever. The words we email, tweet or update on Facebook take on a life of their own as soon as you hit "enter." If you share positive messages or words of encouragement with your tweets and emails, that message (your voice) can take on a life of its own and continue a ripple to many others.

Not that you should need any reason to prevent spreading negative messages and energy with your words, but consider that once your message leaves your fingertips, it takes off like a pigeon to never return. It could live on forever.

Technological advancements in communication have many consequences. Negative energy spread with your actions and words used to die the instant you stopped speaking or moving. Now, it can spread and live on indefinitely. Similarly, an act of kindness or beauty toward another can also spread and perform wonders in the world for ages after you commit the act.

This phenomenon doesn't just happen with electronic communication, though that has certainly increased the impact. The reaching implications of our words and actions have existed since communication began. When you commit an act within your sphere of action, that act will have an effect on those around you, those within your immediate sphere. But when those affected turn around and share your words, your Sphere of Action grows.

I recently saw a video on YouTube that demonstrated this. For six minutes, the video showed how one kind act influenced another kind act from the first recipient or an admiring bystander. The chain of events continued for 20 or 30 iterations until 50 or more people were affected by one first act of kindness.

Maybe this video was dramatized, but it illustrates a valid point. When someone does something kind for you, you are likely inspired to do something kind for another—whether you do so consciously or not. Your action has the ability to inspire the next action, and the next, and the next.... Think of this ripple effect the next time you are faced with an opportunity to either yell at someone for his or her failure or thank them for their best effort; to ignore someone in need or to lend a helping-hand.

When a teacher or parent does something wonderful and influences the life of a child, a ripple of effects is created as the child continues to grow and be influenced by those former actions. They are then able to touch others in the positive way that they were once reached.

This happens on a more immediate scale as well. When you greet people with a wonderful emission of positive energy, you will often leave that person with a smile and positive feeling. When that person encounters others throughout their day, the positive energy that began with you will now be spread to the third party. This ripple effect can continue for many iterations. When we include the secondary, tertiary and beyond effects of our words and actions, we can see just how far our Sphere of Action can actually extend.

Remember that what you put out into the world is what you will also then attract. Wouldn't you prefer your impact to be a positive one?

Flight Delay

Nothing can stop the man with the right mental attitude from achieving his goal; nothing on earth can help the man with the wrong mental attitude.

— THOMAS JEFFERSON

A FEW YEARS AGO, I was flying from North Carolina to Auburn, Alabama. Because of a delay in my first leg, I arrived at my layover 40 minutes late and missed my connecting flight. I found myself delayed for three hours as I waited for the next available flight to my destination. This inconvenience, which seemed like a major deal at the time, would cause so many consequences in my day.

It was a delay that meant I would have to change my car reservation, I would lose valuable work time, and I wouldn't have a chance to go for a stress-reducing run that evening, as I had intended. I would have to drive into Auburn, a town where I had never been, when it was dark, something I had purposely wanted to avoid. I would also likely arrive too late to join anyone for dinner.

The more I thought about it, the longer the list of consequences seemed to grow. I was feeling every sense of frustration most would in this circumstance. The dark thoughts were rolling in, and I could sense an aggravating rest of my day ahead.

Fortunately, I had my understanding of the Spheres to fall back on. I caught myself heading toward this cliff of despair and remembered that I had all the tools I needed to find the positive in this situation. I knew that only I could take control of my Action Sphere and influence the rest of my day as a result.

As I began to analyze my situation more thoroughly, I remembered I was beginning to feel a bit hungry. Had I arrived on time, I would have only had a few moments at the airport to rush to my connecting flight. There would have been no time to grab a bite or use the restroom.

I then remembered how much I actually enjoy spending time at this particular airport, more so than any other I airport I can recall. I decided I could use the extra time I had to stretch my legs while I strolled over to the concourse where someone is usually playing a piano. This would be a great place to sit and finish a book I was reading, take a few notes in my journal, and maybe grab a cup of coffee while I relaxed.

Once I found a few positive aspects of this unexpected layover, each frustration and inconvenience I was anticipating began to seem less significant. While thinking more positively, I reminded myself of the belief that everything in life happens for a reason. Instead of being aggravated now, I was becoming a little curious about what the reason for my delay might be; I embraced the adventure I suddenly found myself on.

I opened my mind and began paying attention to the benefits of this delay. Reasons for this event began to bloom around me. I met a few interesting people, had the chance to do a little shopping, got some exercise by strolling through the terminals, caught up with my dad on the phone, and enjoyed a great espresso. Instead of the frustration and anxiety from this delay dragging me down and creating ripples in the rest of my day, the experience completely renewed my feelings of positive energy.

When I look back at it, that surprise three-hour layover in Charlotte was a gift from the Universe. I was forced to relax, slow down and find my balance. My rush was over, and I now had time to kill. I dealt with all the negative thoughts that were penetrating my Spheres by recognizing the gift I had been given and making the most of my situation.

Not many years before, prior to my education in the tools and management of my Spheres, I am sure experiencing a similar bout of "bad luck" would have left me feeling negative and frustrated, so much so that I wouldn't even have been able to recognize all these positives I gained.

Before I knew and understood the Law of Polarity, I would have only seen the added complications my missed connection created, and not known to look for the coexisting positives. Lacking knowledge of the Laws of Cause and Effect and Vibration, I would not have cared about protecting my vibration or the resulting actions and words expressed during my sour mood.

Here, I was aware that both positive and negative energy perpetuates in self-reinforcing cycles. Trying to prevent my day from becoming any worse, I knew I had to find a way to reestablish a positive emotional energy. I had to prevent my funk from inspiring more negative thoughts, which would inspire poor interactions with those around me, only creating more negative results and frustrations to add to the pile.

What I do know is that the three-hour delay did cause me to arrive at my hotel much later than I had intended. I later realized that had I arrived at my original intended time, I would have been stuck driving in rush hour traffic. And when I did eventually arrive at the hotel, my room had just become available. If I'd arrived three hours earlier, it could have meant three hours of sitting in the lobby, guarding my suitcase. My original plan would have worked out terribly. Instead, that delay provided me with a pleasant drive and a room that was ready when I arrived.

Earlier that day, I chose to respond to events with positive thoughts and actions. What I could control within my Action Sphere was my response of gratitude for the opportunity to breathe a little, rather than reacting in frustration and anger at being majorly inconvenienced. As a result, I was able to embrace a happier me and use the power of my mind to be a positive energy creator and to see the many things I had to be happy for. Had I not changed my perspective through managing my spheres, I would not have been tuned to look for these positive consequences. The delay, it turned out, was an unexpected gift that resulted in nothing but additional positive energy to my day.

With the tools I had and the perspective of finding the positive, I stopped that potential downward spiral in my day. When I got back on the plane for the next leg, I was reenergized and had a satisfied stomach. Who knows how the conversations I had and the people I met may have affected my future. Did I make a connection with a potential friend? Did something I learned in conversation, or through my observations in the concourse, affect my future actions in some way? Maybe the only long-term benefit from this experience was having the story to share with you in this book.

If that is the case, it was well worth it.

Section Two

◎

Bite-Size Recap

T HE LAW OF CAUSE AND EFFECT tells us that the energy you put out into the world, through your actions and deeds, is the same energy that is reflected back to you. When you put out positive energy, you will create an environment around you of positive energy. Your smile, your compliments and your kind gestures toward others will spread this positive energy in the emotions they develop.

Every interaction we have with other people, no matter how fleeting or insignificant, creates a change in their energy state in some way. When we smile as we pass someone on the street, this creates a positive energy increase for them, even if just by an iota. The connection for that one second makes them feel noticed and significant. A genuine smile is an indication that their impression is favorable and that they aren't being negatively judged. Even if this fleeting connection does not spread much (or any) positive energy, it is at least a brief experience that doesn't compound any negative emotions that they presently hold. Sometimes, just stopping a person from a moment of progress on a downward emotional spiral is enough to count the moment as a win.

In the same way, every negative action we demonstrate toward others, no matter how small or insignificant we believe these actions to be, can have a negative effect on that person. The shortest moment of rudeness or judgment when passing another in the hallway can distribute your negative emotional energy. If we snap a rude comment or shove our way past someone in a busy room, this will negatively affect their energy and bring their vibration down a little. Even an insignificant passing of someone in the street with no connection may affect another because we feed an insecurity in them by acting as though they aren't important or noticeable.

We are always creating and emitting some kind of emotional energy. As a result, our interactions are always affecting those around us. We are either increasing or decreasing the energy of everyone we encounter.

Wouldn't you rather be known as the person who brightens a room and leaves people feeling a little more cheerful, instead of being known as someone who passes through life making no impact at all?

Be the person who brings a little positive energy into every situation. What better way could there possibly be to live?

Purposeful or Useful

I typically hold to the belief that everything in life happens for a reason. When I am frustrated by an event that occurs, I ease my frustration by searching for the reason it may have happened. What did I gain from it? How was my day or my life altered by that experience and how am I now on a better path?

My friend Bob Kodzis[1] once shared with me his belief that things don't happen for a reason but everything that happens is useful. Things you have experienced may not have transpired for a reason, but there is always something from that experience that will be useful in the future. If you want to quell your anger or frustration from something you have faced, find a way to make that experience useful!

- **Indirect Sphere:** Largest Sphere, consisting of all events and circumstances that are outside our control and have no direct influence over us (i.e. an earthquake in another country where we know no one.)

- **Direct Sphere:** All events and circumstances that directly affect us which we must either respond or react to (i.e. being a victim of identity theft.)

- **Action Sphere:** Everything in the world we can affect ourselves (i.e. the tone of the conversation you have with your child in the morning, prior to sending him or her off to school.)

Remember that while the Indirect Sphere does not directly affect us, it can have an affect over us if we allow it to. Devoting too much time to worrying about an earthquake in another country means less time to devote to Direct and Action Sphere concerns.

Similarly, while we cannot control the events and circumstances that occur within the Direct Sphere, we can control how we respond to those events and circumstances. For instance, getting into a car accident is never fun for anyone, but responding aggressively or dwelling on the frustration could certainly make the incident worse.

---

1   Bob Kodzis is President and Chief Creative Catalyst at Flight of Ideas, Inc. This organization is a "creative think-tank that helps groups think out of the tank." Find out more at www.flightofideas.net

Our responses to events in the Direct Sphere extend into the Action Sphere through the impact our actions have on those we connect with.

By reducing the energy we give to Indirect Sphere events and circumstances, and using the Universal Laws to find positive ways to react to Direct Sphere events and circumstances, we can shrink each of those Spheres and increase the energy we have to devote to our Action Sphere—thereby increasing the positive impact we can have on the world around us and the positive results we then attract to us.

Section Two

---------- ◎ ----------

Applying What You've Learned

30 Days Of Gratitude

I N THE SECTION ON Using Your Action Sphere, we discussed the influence gratitude can have over our vibrations. It is a powerful tool to apply during times of despair and helplessness when you need to find ways to turn your vibration around. Gratitude can also be a great way to maintain a highly positive frequency during good times.

So, I want to challenge you to make gratitude a priority over the next 30 days. Commit five minutes every day to reflecting upon all you have to be grateful for. This exercise is more powerful if you write those items down, so consider getting yourself a gratitude notebook for just that purpose.

Some people may find these reflections most beneficial at the start of their day, beginning on a positive note, while others may prefer to make this exercise the last thing they do each night. The timing of your reflections does not matter, so long as you maintain your commitment to making this a routine part of your day.

Remember that you don't have to reflect upon big things every day in order for that gratitude to have an effect. Yes, getting married or having a child can be incredible boosts to our positive vibration—but these are not things that occur every day. Be willing to find the blessings in the smaller aspects of your day as well. Typical items for your gratitude journal might include:

- The barista who knew your order before you said a word.
- The praise you received from a coworker for a job well done.
- The time you got to spend having lunch with an old friend.
- The car you have to get you to and from work.
- The good night's rest you were able to achieve.

You don't have to go big in order for your gratitude to matter. You just have to be willing to reflect upon the many things within your life you have to be grateful for.

As you complete this exercise, I want you to pay attention to how it helps to improve your overall well-being and positive emotions. Most people find that a dedicated focus on gratitude eases stress and improves happiness—so much so, that you may find this is an exercise you want to continue even after your 30 days.

Identify And Manage That Sphere

I'VE GIVEN YOU a lot of examples of how best to manage various events and circumstances occurring within each of these Spheres, but these examples are all abstract until you find ways to apply them to your own life. This is why I want to encourage you to spend three days actively paying attention to the events and circumstances affecting your own life, determining which Sphere they are related to, and intentionally using the Laws to navigate them in the most positive way possible.

With time, much of this can become second nature. But in the beginning, it takes practice and dedication to identify the Spheres and manage them effectively, which is where this exercise comes in—it is the first step in increasing your own awareness.

Start by writing yourself reminders that you will see throughout your day to check in on your Spheres. Post-it notes in your bathroom, on the dashboard of your car and in a planner might be a good place to start. Truly, something as simple as "Check in with your Spheres!" can be enough of a reminder to get your head where it needs to be when those events and circumstances arise.

Then, pay attention to those events and circumstances that inspire a response from you throughout the day. Examples might be:

- Getting a call from a gossipy relative who wants to let you in on the latest dramas a distant cousin is dealing with (Indirect Sphere).
- Being told by your boss that you need to work this weekend, even though you already have plans with your family (Direct Sphere).
- Making the decision to contribute some of your free time to volunteering with Habitat for Humanity, as in working with your hands and helping to make a home for a disadvantaged family has always been a passion of yours (Action Sphere).

As these occurrences come up and weigh on your mind, ask yourself these questions:

- Is this something that directly affects me?
- Do I have to respond to this?
- If I do have to respond, what is the most positive way to do so?
- Can I make a difference in this situation, and would making that difference positively or negatively affect me?

Remember, if an event or circumstance does not directly affect you and does not require a response on your end, it is likely an Indirect Sphere item—meaning that your energy is best spent finding ways to no longer dwell on that event or circumstance. (Even if that means finding a way to get off the phone with your gossipy relative!)

For Direct Sphere events and circumstances, try using the Universal Laws as you attempt to respond in ways that will positively impact you and those around you.

And always remember that when you are impacting those around you, it is an extension of your Action Sphere—and those impacts have the potential to be far reaching. So, always aim to make that mark a positive one.

Bonus Challenge: Take on this challenge with a partner. For the three days, commit to emailing your reflections to each other—discussing and evaluating the different Spheres involved and your attempts to minimize both the Indirect and Direct Spheres while increasing the positive impact of your Action Sphere. Having that partner to hold you accountable and help you increase your understanding of these ideas can greatly enhance your ability to grasp these new concepts and begin making long-term changes in how you approach the world around you.

Section Three:
Putting it All Together

Chapter 5

─────────── ◎ ───────────

Clouds in Our Sky

B Y NOW, WE'VE TALKED a lot about the Spheres, how to manage them, and how they relate to one another. The next step is learning how to apply these lessons to your own life.

It isn't uncommon to go through life wishing we had more time to devote to the things that really matter to us. When we learn to let go of the things we cannot control, we have taken a major leap in recapturing some of our own time and energy—time and energy we can then use more effectively in other realms of our life. That starts with identifying what events and circumstances lay beyond our Direct Sphere. Just this acknowledgement may be enough to let go of certain worries and concerns which are slowing us down.

Let's imagine all those outside distractions we can't control as being the dark clouds skewing our focus—then let's talk about how to wipe those dark clouds away.

If you found yourself standing in the middle of a green pasture or on a beautiful white sand beach, picture the sky as being representative of your mind. When we allow negative thoughts and emotions to enter our mind, they can have the same effect as dark rain clouds in our sky. A few dark clouds are not enough to keep us from enjoying the sun that shines through, but if we can get rid of all the clouds, we might enjoy the day more fully.

Imagine you are sitting on the beach with your family some afternoon and a single dark cloud enters your periphery. A dark cloud in your mind can draw your focus and attention. Instead of enjoying the breeze, playing with your kids or reading a book, you stare at that dark cloud. You wonder if it is going to bring more rain or if you should start to pack up your things. You fret and complain, convinced that one cloud is going to ruin your vacation, instead of simply enjoying the beauty offered by everything else around you.

Let's take this scene a little further. Imagine more dark clouds continuing to enter your beautiful sky and rain becoming inevitable. If the sky fills with rain clouds, it blocks out all the rays of sun you were previously enjoying. When the rain begins to pour, you can do nothing but bow your head and protect yourself from that rain. If the rain picks up and the wind begins to blow, the best you can manage is to hurry around in a panic with your face toward the ground as you deal with everything you have to pack up. Your attention is focused solely on the task of gathering your things and trying to get away from the rain. If there is no shelter nearby, your only choice is to keep your head bowed and struggle to find a solution and hope the rain soon passes.

This cloud analogy can be similar to thoughts in our mind. When the sky is clear, we experience a peaceful and calm life. We enjoy the things going on around us, we appreciate the blessings we have and we get the most from each day.

Now imagine the positive things in your world are like rays of sunshine. If you are effectively managing your Spheres, you should have a sky full of sunshine and white puffy clouds. As dark rain clouds enter your sky, new rays of sunshine dissolve them, just as a happy thought or a joyful moment can negate a concern or frustration weighing on your mind.

Many things can provide sources of these dark clouds in our sky. The news on television, events from our past and our interactions with others can all provide dark clouds. So how do you combat those clouds and invite in the sun?

The News

W E ARE A NATION OBSESSED with the news. The 24-hour news cycle continuously fuels our consciousness with the latest click-worthy titles, keeping us in the loop about stories from around the world. We often feel as though we need to stay plugged in to ensure we are always in the know about what is going on. We never want to feel left out, and we convince ourselves all this news is important and that we must remain informed.

I'm going to let you in on a little secret. I have joined a growing number of individuals who personally refrain from watching the news as much as I can. What I have found is that very little, if anything, in the news brings actual value to my life.

I initially experimented by giving up the news for a few weeks. The time I saved was soon devoured by the many other things I found I would rather be doing. Even more profound, it quickly occurred to me that my lack of indulgence in clicking through news websites or zoning out in front of the television wasn't costing me anything. I wasn't missing out on anything important to me. I really enjoyed spending that time doing other things, like hanging out with family and friends, reading a book, visiting the park, and even (especially!) writing this book.

After my short reprieve from the news, I noticed another interesting thing. My mind wasn't consumed by the many negative stories and tragedies that typically overwhelm news headlines. I had always previously allowed the news to play in the background as I got ready for work or cleaned up around the house. But now, I realized that without that negativity forever permeating the background of my life, I wasn't just saving time, I was also protecting my own vibration.

Once I stopped the flow of these negative sound bites into my mind, I found my thoughts consumed by other things. Instead of recounting those news stories with friends, my conversations tended toward more positive and productive topics. The hours previously spent dwelling on murder sprees, train crashes, stock market blips and any other hot news stories with friends and coworkers turned to time spent sharing a book I had read or an interesting idea for a weekend trip.

I am not saying you need to give up watching the news entirely. How you spend your time is your decision. But if you remember that Indirect Sphere events have the tendency to draw dark clouds in our proverbial sky, you may find you are best served by eliminating those clouds entirely so that you can increase your own sunshine.

You are likely asking yourself, *what if something happens that I need to know?* Chances are, if anything occurs in the world that will enter your Direct Sphere, you aren't going to first hear about it on the news. If you are going to lose your job, if your marriage or friendships are in jeopardy, or if your health is deteriorating, you won't find that story on the public news station. This information will come to you in other, more direct ways. If there are certain interests in your life that you would like to be informed about, set up some Google Alerts so you receive just the information about the stories or topics that are important to you. Set an alert about your hometown, the school you attend or the business you work for, the sports teams you like, et cetera. With this approach, you won't miss out on the stories you care about, but you will filter from your mind the continuous feed of negative news stories of murders, crashes, bankruptcies and celebrity tragedies that fill the news websites, television news feeds and the pages of the paper.

When a tragic event does occur like a factory explosion, a train derailment or hurricane that is affecting another part of the country, these Indirect Sphere events can take a toll on our emotional state, but they also present an opportunity to inspire us.

The negative vibration we feel after indulging in horrific stories on the news is often a symptom of helplessness to do anything about the situation or to prevent such an event from happening in our own lives. By taking action and contributing our time or money to support the victims of tragic event, we can turn the influence of a negative event into an empowering one.

Whenever a major tragedy occurs, there is always a way to chip in and contribute to the cause. After Hurricane Katrina, medical professionals and students from around the county traveled to New Orleans to volunteer their time and services. Following the recent disaster in Haiti, many people traveled to help. For those who couldn't contribute their time or afford the expense, many enjoyed making a difference by donating a few dollars to help the efforts. Instead of allowing the news to haunt your thoughts and emotions, find a way to help and enjoy the good feeling of knowing you made a difference for someone in need.

While I talk primarily about the negative effects of indulging in too much news, the news isn't the only television broadcast that can have tragic ramifications on our thoughts, emotions and mood.

There was a period in my life where I got in the routine of working hard all day, coming home and doing some work around the house and then sitting down and watching a few episodes of *Law and Order*. This was around the time that my cable company began offering a digital video recorder, which I programmed to record any episode of *Law and Order* that aired on television. As a result, I always had one or two reruns of *L & O* to watch when I sat down to veg out each evening.

What I came to realize, with my understanding of how external stimuli effect my internal emotions and thoughts, was that watching two or more hours a day of stories about murder, rape, corruption and robbery certainly wasn't the best use of my time. True, I did know that the stories, though seemingly familiar and realistic, were all fictional. But, as we discussed before, these fictional stories had the same ability to influence my emotions, thereby affecting the way I would think, feel and act. Do I have a specific example of how these hours of exposure to television drama conditioned my thoughts? Not really. But I am certain they did not have a positive effect on my psyche.

Don't get me wrong; I have nothing personally against *Law and Order*. I still think it is one of the greatest shows to have ever been produced. But indulging in socially disturbing episodes and violence certainly wasn't doing any favors to the way I saw the world and the vibration I maintained.

I still watch television on occasion, and I always enjoy going to the movies. I like the emotional rollercoaster, and I am not advocating that people give up all indulgence in television, movies or a good fiction book. Just be conscientious of the messages you are allowing into your mind. Do you overindulge in murder-mysteries? Does the music you listen to portray hateful lyrics or a victim-of- circumstance message?

Be careful what you allow to pass into your periphery. Everything we hear, see or feel has the ability to condition us in some way, the ability to affect our subconscious thoughts and our emotions. How would you like to be affected? `

I mention the news, television dramas and the negativity they can bring as the first topic in this section because it illustrates one of the most basic principles of managing our Spheres. If there is a source of dark, stormy rain clouds consistently casting shadows on your mind and providing a source of negative energy, cut that source out of your life. There are enough items to attend to in your Direct Sphere; things deserving of all the attention and energy you have to give. When your emotions are worn by the concerns on your mind that come from the Indirect Sphere, you are jeopardizing the energy you can devote to anything else.

If we don't deal with the dark clouds in our Indirect Sphere, they have the ability to flow into our Direct Sphere and really take a toll. If your mind is consumed by negative energy from things beyond your direct influence, there is too great a chance for you to create an environment for Direct Sphere things to pile up against you. If a negative story on the news distracts your attention while getting ready for work or while driving to the office, it may slow you down and cause you to be late to work. Or it may consume your attention and contribute to your being in an accident. Now you have some Direct Sphere things to contend with, things you must actually manage.

If your mind is burdened by the tragic news of a recent oil spill or a tumble in the economy (which doesn't actually threaten the job you have), this will likely affect the attitude you have around your friends or the attention you devote to your family.

Let that trend continue long enough and you will certainly have some Direct Sphere consequences—all created by those Indirect Sphere dark clouds.

When this energy from the Indirect Sphere is creating consequences in our Direct Sphere, it is because we have allowed this influence, this dark cloud, to move into our Direct Sphere. Draw the line in the sand. Determine what belongs in the Indirect Sphere, those events and circumstances that wouldn't have a direct effect on your life unless you allowed them to, and push them out of your life. Guard your Direct Sphere to protect these dark clouds from flowing through.

The Past

W E DISCUSSED THE PAST a bit in the introduction to the Indirect Sphere already, but when it comes to those dark clouds created by the past, where do we draw the line between the Indirect and Direct Spheres?

We all have circumstances that have resided in our Direct Sphere for so long that we may begin to feel as though they belong there. And once upon a time, maybe they did. But in most cases, issues from the past should have long since moved to the Indirect Sphere where they no longer direct our thoughts, attention and actions. Many times, it is simply our clinging to the past that keeps it alive in our minds.

Remember that the goal for managing our Spheres, though, is to shrink that Direct Sphere, to move things from directly affecting us to the appropriate place where they no longer affect our lives. Consequences from past errors we have made may still exist today, but thoughts that dwell in our minds from past mistakes no longer need to reside in our attention. Consequences that we face today are no more than a starting point toward a brighter future. Gilt, frustration, concern and regret are just negative emotions that keep us from moving beyond our current circumstances to a better tomorrow. Everything that happened in the past happened for a reason. Learn the lesson you can from it, be grateful it didn't kill you, and use the experience you gained to move forward.

To do this, we need to address the dark clouds that are hiding in our Direct Sphere, the things that we are allowing to directly affect us, even though they shouldn't. Often, these things are events from the past, and the time has come for us to move beyond them.

To deal with these concerns, we can use the Universal Laws to find positives we didn't see before. We can also reflect on the nature of many of these dark clouds we have let in, working to recognize that they no longer need to directly affect us. One of the quickest remedies for this new perspective is to remember that there is nothing we can do to change the past. Mistakes that we have made, regrets we contend with, friends who have hurt us, events that have affected us or created the circumstances we see today... there is nothing we can do change them. No matter how much energy we expend or frustration we hold, we cannot undo anything that has already transpired. The best we can do is learn the lessons we were meant to learn and stop allowing these things to reside in our Direct Sphere. The longer this negative energy festers, the more damage it will do to our lives, affecting the actions we take today and the energy we have to devote toward our dreams and ambitions for tomorrow.

The same can be true for the negative events from our past. When we allow ourselves to remain entangled in those past events, they pound away at us and distract from the present. But when we let them go, realizing there is nothing we can do to change what has already happened, we free up energy to directly affect our current situation.

We have all done things in the past we wish we hadn't. We have each made decisions or taken actions that produced results we weren't happy with. This can happen to us on the small, short-term scale, or over the much broader and longer lasting picture. We may wish we had not made that impulse buy that drained our savings, or that we hadn't eaten all the food we did over the weekend. Perhaps we wish we had gotten more sleep last night or gotten out of bed a little earlier this morning. Maybe we are filled with regret, wishing we hadn't acted a certain way in a relationship or yearning to take back something we said to a friend. On a grander scale, there may be certain career decisions we would love the chance to do over. Or a dream opportunity we wish we could go back and accept.

I know that I have personally made many mistakes in my life. I have done some things for which I am not proud. I have hurt feelings, and had my own hurt in return. I have made decisions on impulse that created consequences I did not intend or desire. I am sure if I were to tally up all the mistakes and regretful actions in my life, I would find that I have embarrassed myself enough times to feel crippled by shame. Instead of allowing this reaction from my past mistakes, I remember the Universal Laws, and I look for the positive, no matter how small, that has come from these missteps, and even at times egregious mistakes.

Every step we have taken along the path we've traveled has brought us to where we are right now. The mistakes we've made were also opportunities to grow stronger and gain experience.

Some lessons are harder learned than others, but every experience, whether good or bad, can make us better for the future.

If you want to see your mistakes as a positive learning experience that has made you better equipped to live today, you can find a way. If you would like to use the embarrassment and humility to make you a better friend and keep you from judging others for their mistakes, that's your choice. If you would like to feel more patience, acceptance and understanding for others because it helps you cultivate and express kindness in your actions, you can gain those traits by reflecting on your own mistakes and failures.

The past will only hold you back from your future if you refuse to let go of it.

> *The pessimist complains about the wind; the optimist expects it to change; the realist adjusts the sails.*
>
> — WILLIAM ARTHUR WARD

Interactions With Others

I USED TO BE MUCH MORE open to listening to those who felt the need to share their woes with me. When I passed someone in the hall who wished to share a frustration, I would allow them the opportunity to indulge for a moment and unload the burden of mind. I once felt I was being helpful by giving them an ear to listen. My ear. That was, until I better understood this relationship between cause and effect and vibration.

Now, I am much less tolerant of, and will even walk away from, casual conversations that veer toward moping or dwelling on the negative—because those conversations can bring dark clouds into my life. If that seems rude or inconsiderate, think about what it says that another person is trying to unload their pain and burden upon you. When they feel a bit of relief from off-loading their frustration, it is because you have taken on some of that burden. Maybe the problem doesn't become your own, but the negative thoughts and emotional energy can certainly be transferred over to you.

Don't misunderstand; I certainly believe it is best to provide a positive influence and ray of sunshine for others whenever possible. I still have compassion toward helping others when I can. I will always invest my time and energy if I believe someone is looking for help and that help is something I can provide. Many times, talking through a problem is the most effective way to find a solution to life's struggles. If I find this to be the intent of a conversation, I am all ears.

What I avoid (and have lost patience for) are people who only discuss their problems with the purpose of wallowing in their grief and making others feel sorry for their pain. I've had coworkers who come in every day with a new "woe is me" story, or worse, a new embellishment of an old one.

I do hurt for people who struggle and can often understand why they feel or act the way they do. I don't have judgment toward them; I just don't see a purpose in jumping into someone's problems with them if they have no intention or desire to change.

I have personally, at times, taken comfort in feelings of despair, anger and depression, so I get the motivation. But you just can't help people at a time when they don't really want help. I have enough challenges and frustrations in my own life; I don't need to indulge my thoughts in someone else's negative energy if it's not for the purpose of progressing to a better future.

When someone does present a frustration or come to you for a helping hand through a trying time, use what you know about the Universal Laws and managing your spheres to help. Help another find the positive in a troubling situation if they are ready to see it. It often requires a friend's perspective of a situation to find the opportunity that accompanies an event or new circumstance. Be that friend whenever you can.

To emphasize why we shouldn't indulge in or listen to idle negative conversation from others, consider an extreme example. If everyone you interacted with at work and throughout your day were to barrage you with his or her personal problems and woes for the sole purpose of sharing their grief, what toll would this take on your own emotional energy? What vibration would you hold tomorrow when a friend comes to you in need of compassion if you spent today unproductively wallowing in the struggles and negative energy of near-strangers passing by?

Now imagine that everyone you met for a few days shared stories of inspiration and positive stories of happiness. What boost would this give to your confidence and positive outlook? Imagine how much stronger would your positive vibration be to deal with your own challenges or to help a friend in need.

By recognizing the impact these interactions can have, we begin to understand how even just the passing morose conversation might chip away at our energy. I'm not saying you should run away and avoid conversations about negative topics when someone is in need of a sounding board. You should absolutely be compassionate and do what you can to help others where you can. And when it comes to close friends and family members, we should likely be even more open and willing. After all, each of us needs people close to us with whom we can share our problems and life concerns—not for the purpose of unloading a burden or garnering sympathy, but as a resource to talk through our problems. There is a difference between a close friend turning to you for advice and a stranger at the checkout line unloading their bad day upon you. So know there will absolutely be occasions when listening to the problems of other people is part of being a good friend and person. But understand the effect such encounters may have on your state of mind, and don't expect to take on the burdens of everyone you encounter—especially if you find yourself in a less than positive vibration already.

You are not responsible for the woes of everyone you meet; you are not responsible to provide occasion for others to indulge in their own pity or idle, negative conversation.

With friends and family members, sometimes you have to evaluate whether the relationship provides more benefit or harm to your life. It is normal for people to want to discuss their problems with close friends, but there are some people who are always dwelling on something negative. A friend who routinely uses you as an outlet to unload their problems, and who never seems willing to make any changes to resolve those issues, is likely not someone whom you should continue enabling by being that resource. At some point, it becomes detrimental to you and to them—which is when it may be time to remove yourself from that relationship.

Give the best of yourself to your friendships and, if it is a good relationship for you to have, you will get the best in return. But don't be afraid to separate yourself from relationships that bring more negative energy than positive into your life.

Remember that negative energy can flow from one person to another. So be selective about whom you allow to unburden their woes to you. Be a resource when you can, but don't sacrifice yourself at the expense of being a shoulder to cry on for everyone else.

Surround yourself with positive people and you'll be a positive person.
— KELLIE PICKLER

Judgment

Don't judge a man until you have walked two moons in his moccasins.
— NATIVE AMERICAN PROVERB

EVERYONE KNOWS WHAT JUDGMENT IS and how bad it can be. We've seen it, we've been the victim of it, and we've perpetuated it. Anytime we determine another person is doing something, or acting in a way they shouldn't be, we are judging them.

We all do it. I have been just as guilty of that tendency toward judging others as the next person. Even so, I work hard to be conscious of it, and I strive to stop myself anytime I feel I may be judging another in thought or in words. Those judgments rarely serve any good purpose, and the act of judgment only provides clouds darkening up our sky.

To judge someone else, you have to first view yourself as superior in some way. While we all have our own strengths and weaknesses, I think the sum of our abilities and traits is about equal. If you are a religious person, why would it not be so? If you believe in a just Universe, how could it be any other way?

Now, some people will flex their talents and pursue their passions and therefore become much brighter and more influential and positive beings, while others may let the demons that reside in all of us take hold and run their life in a direction of disgust or despair. All of us are born with the same potential to pursue our passion and fulfill our highest ability or purpose—like identical seeds planted in the soil. Some seek water and sunlight and grow into beautiful flowers. Others find darkness and moist ground and become overtaken by fungus and mold. Either way, we all have the potential for greatness and for despair.

I am blessed to have recognized and overcome many challenges in my life, and I feel good about the path I am now on. Still, I know I just as easily could have succumbed to various temptations and wound up on a different road. But for a small margin, I had all the potential for a life of drugs or violence or crime or poverty—the same path that more than a few childhood friends chose.

The truth is, were any of us to have lived a life in another person's shoes, we could very well have ended up exactly where they are.

> *There but for the grace of God go I.*
> — JOHN BRADFORD

Judgment, in general, is a poison. It spawns from feelings of superiority in some measure and is the foundation for gossip, which only promotes and perpetuates more judgment. But judgment is also so often the unhealthy expression of insecurity, which only aims to level the playing field by knocking others off their perceived pedestals. When we are engaged in such negative thoughts and actions, we are only inviting that negativity back unto ourselves.

Remember the Laws—you get back what you put out.

Before passing judgment on another, I try to remember that I too have made many mistakes, been an ass many times, and hurt others more than I care to admit. Then I remind myself that anyone I may be on the cusp of judging has likely also made many contributions and done many good deeds—at least to the best of their ability.

Intent goes a long way. If you are genuinely pointing out another person's errors or missteps in an attempt to help them, rather than judge them, that same negativity does not exist. But that requires skill, compassion and care. For another to benefit from your words, you have to create a change of thought within their minds. As the old adage goes, "A man convinced against his will is of the same opinion still."

In general, our judgment of others will only attract to us more dark clouds. Remembering that all people are human and that we all have the propensity for falls from grace is perhaps the best way to extinguish those clouds and go through life with a greater aim of positively affecting those around us.

If things in your life have not manifest as you desired, then accept that circumstances are just not as you would like, but embrace your full power to change them moving forward. Release your frustration over the past and present without tempering your resolve for creating a brighter future.

The same goes for dealing with people. If people in your life do not act the way you would like or find interest in the things you wish they would, then accept them for their differences and appreciate their uniqueness. If you encounter people with a negative attitude, or those who act unkindly toward you, realize they do so because of their own insecurities, negative emotions and frustrations. Accept their character and actions as something for them to contend with, not you. If they are a dark rain cloud in your life, then be a source of positive light or remove them from your Direct Sphere and extinguish their influence over you.

Accept things and people for the way they are, and accept them for the way they are not.

Forgiveness

ONE MAJOR GHOST from the Indirect Sphere that can cloud our skies is the issue of forgiveness.

Each of us has been hurt, likely many times throughout our lives. People have wronged us, harmed us, lied to us and betrayed us. It is part of the human condition—learning that every person is fallible and that sometimes even innocent bystanders become collateral damage to that fallibility.

We are all broken. However, it is often through those cracks that the light is let in.

The key is in learning to forgive, even when that forgiveness feels foreign or undeserved. In fact, one of the greatest roadblocks to achieving a happy future is the inability to forgive those who have hurt us. Even the inability to forgive ourselves for past transgressions can weigh heavily on our minds. Withholding forgiveness can create a dark cloud in our spheres, making it nearly impossible to see past the hurt and move forward to a brighter place.

Everyone makes mistakes in life. What we sometimes forget, though, is that most people are just doing the best they can. There are only a few truly nasty people in the world who act with intentional malice. The rest of us are inherently decent people with varying degrees of "good" and "bad" struggling within us.

We each have the propensity to treat others well. We each also have the ability to act in ways that are selfish and cruel. We are all capable of making mistakes, and those mistakes come with consequences. Sometimes, they are consequences we pay for ourselves, and sometimes others pay the consequences as a result of our mistakes or poor choices.

The point is, we all have consequences to deal with. Maybe you made a mistake in the past that set you back a few years. (Or at least, you perceived it to set you back.) In those cases, it is important to remember that setbacks and heartbreaks, whether a result of our own missteps or those of others, can bring us to exactly where we are meant to be. It is hard to accept at times, but mistakes and lapses of judgment are a part of life. They are a part of the growing experience. Surviving our errors in judgment and the wrongs others have committed against us is part of what makes us who we are; it is all a piece of the puzzle creating the life we now live.

Each of us has a different journey to travel to get to where we are going in life. Some of our pasts are more littered and clouded with mistakes than others, but that is part of living a unique life. When we make mistakes that we are able to learn from, that is when we grow and become better versions of ourselves. Without those missteps, we would never evolve.

So when you have been hurt, either by yourself or by another, take the time to really examine the situation for the lessons that can be learned from it. There is value to be found in even the most traumatic of experiences. And when you can find the way an event falls into the bigger puzzle of your life, it becomes much easier to accept and move beyond the hurt itself.

What did you learn? What did you not understand or suspect before that you now know for certain? What error in judgment did you make that cost you a small price today but taught you a lesson that will prevent you from possibly making a much larger mistake in the future? How can you now be a better friend or parent with what you have learned?

Seek the positives from every situation—even those in which you were wronged. And cut yourself some slack for those times when you were the offender. That doesn't mean taking free rein to hurt others in the future; it means learning from those mistakes and using them to grow into a better person moving forward. Don't allow those mistakes to become the definition of who you are. Grow from them, and help others to do the same. Be honest with your kids, fess up to your close friends and own your past when it comes to talking to your significant other.

As for those who have hurt us, those situations can vary broadly. People affect us in different ways all the time. We may have different expectations of those we encounter, from close friends to distant acquaintances. There will be times when the wounds inflicted upon us by others are barely noticeable. And other times the pain caused by someone we hold dear feels like a dagger in the back, particularly when we are hurt by those we least expected to hurt us. It is in those instances when we tend to hold on to our anger and frustration most tightly. That lack of forgiveness can plague us for a lifetime.

The more severe the wrong, the more imperative it is for you to forgive. Understand, forgiveness does not always mean allowing a person to continue bearing control over your life and emotions. Maybe they no longer need to be a part of your life; most certainly their prior actions and the burden you carry no longer have to be. Forgiveness doesn't mean giving them the chance to hurt you again. It just means letting go of the hurt you feel and accepting that it was a part of your life; a small piece of the larger puzzle.

If you can't seem to forgive a person because you feel their actions were purposeful or too severe, then do the best you can to at least move on. Separate them from your life and continue forward. Forgive yourself for being in the situation that allowed you to be hurt. And remember that you inevitably learned something that can help you in the future.

Do the learning and then let it go.

Chapter 6

—————————————— ◎ ——————————————

Taking Control

S O, HOW DO YOU ULTIMATELY MANAGE all these dark clouds in your sky? Well, it starts with asking yourself—do I have a choice in whether or not this affects me?

This may be a difficult question to answer truthfully at first look. Plenty of things cause emotional responses in our body and mind that tie an event or circumstance to us directly. Like the movie we spoke about earlier, even fictitious characters in a made up story can have an effect on our emotions, leaving us either depressed or inspired. This happens even when we are fully aware that the story we are taking in is fake. But the real question here is, does it have to affect us?

And what can we do to push those dark clouds away when this first attempt doesn't work?

OODA Loop

To let life happen to you is irresponsible. To create
your day is your divine right.

— RAMTHA

The OODA Loop is a term coined by military strategist, Lieutenant Colonel Boyd. It is an understanding of human and group cognitive behavior used to strategize actions against an enemy in combat. While it is a term that is likely unfamiliar to those outside of the military community, I think it applies very effectively to each of us by giving us a framework to analyze the events and circumstances in our lives.

OODA is an acronym for a four-step process: **Observe, Orient, Decide,** and **Act.** This is the normal cycle of cognitive actions we go through when faced with an event or circumstance in our lives. The OODA Loop is a continuous process that we repeat with every new stimulus we encounter.

To **Observe**, we witness or acknowledge something happening around us. Every sound, motion, feeling or taste we experience is an observation. Our brain can do this in our subconscious without us even realizing it is happening. We are constantly in a state of observing.

Once we have observed something, we **Orient** ourselves to that observation. We determine if the observation will affect us, and if so, how. Does the thing or event we observed present a danger? Do we need to take action in order to respond to, compensate for, or avoid the thing or event we observed?

After we orient ourselves to an event that has occurred or a circumstance we have encountered, we **Decide** what, if anything, we need to do about it. During this decision, we will weigh our potential options for action and consider the potential consequences of each action. Maybe we see a leaf falling in the distance. We observe the leaf, orient ourselves to it, and decide no further action is required. However, if we observe a tree branch falling from a tree we are standing beneath, we might orient ourselves to this branch and decide it is a threat that we must move away from.

If a decision is made that we must do something, the last step of the loop is to **Act** on that decision. Thus, you step out of the way of the branch before it strikes us.

The OODA Loop is recognized as a loop because it never ends. Once you've taken an action, the situation has changed and this new situation requires another observation. In the case of the falling tree branch, maybe you take an action to jump out of the way. Once you have jumped, you must observe the falling branch again to ensure you have cleared its path. Once you orient your new position to this still falling branch, you may decide that you are fine or that you must move again. Either way, you then you act accordingly.

Think of yourself driving a vehicle on the freeway. As other vehicles on the road maneuver around you, you **Observe** the motion of those vehicles. You **Orient** yourself to them (are they near your vehicle or far away, are they approaching from the left side or the right). You then **Decide** what, if anything, you must do to compensate for the other vehicles on the road—slow down, turn, change lanes, or maintain speed—and then you **Act** on this new information.

In the military sense, commanders attempt to disrupt the OODA Loop of their enemy. They strategize how they can change the situation on the battlefield so rapidly that an enemy cannot effectively complete their OODA Loop. If a commander is successful at disrupting the enemy's OODA Loop, they gain an advantage. The enemy is stuck in this cognitive loop, unable to make an effective decision; they cannot respond quickly enough to what they last observed before they must make another observation and orientation. In the time it takes the enemy to make a decision regarding one observation, the opposing commander's troops have already taken another action requiring another OODA Loop entirely.

Imagine this concept of the OODA Loop in a basketball game. Visualize a basketball player dribbling a ball down the court. As he approaches a defending opponent from the other team, he stops dribbling and may pretend he is going to pass the ball. As this player motions to attempt that pass, the defender *observes* this action and *orients* himself to what he believes will take place.

How far is the opponent currently standing from the passer? Who might the player with the ball pass to? Is that teammate who may receive the pass moving? Are they in a position to take a shot?

Once oriented to the situation, this defender will *decide* what he should do in order to prevent the pass, block a shot or steal the ball. Once the decision is made, this defender will *act*.

If you imagine this scene playing out in your mind, you can begin to appreciate just how fast this OODA Loop can progress. Each time the player with the ball hints at another action, this defender's OODA Loop must begin again. If he fakes a pass to the left, then the right, then looks to the basket as though he were going to shoot the ball, this would require the defender to conduct three separate OODA Loops, all in the matter of one to two seconds.

Just like the commander on the battlefield, the player holding the ball will attempt to disrupt his opponent's OODA Loop by preventing the time to orient effectively, or to act decisively. Once the OODA Loop is effectively disrupted, the player with the ball maintains the advantage.

Whether we are aware of it or not, our minds are continuously managing a multitude of OODA Loops at the same time. Some loops are conducted in a matter of seconds—every sound we hear or motion we see may require an OODA Loop in our subconscious mind. Some OODA Loops are extended beyond days or months. Maybe we observe something at work, orient ourselves to what this observation means and what options it presents, then we decide on an action and act upon it. Whether the loop takes a fraction of a second or months to complete, nearly every action we take is the result of some cognitive decision our mind makes after following this process.

In our normal, low-stress and routine lives, this process tends to work brilliantly. But when we are overloaded and stressed, that Loop may come off the track. Being tired, anxious, or overworked can cause the OODA Loop to malfunction and force us to begin missing steps in the loop. When we fail to properly complete this cognitive process, we may find ourselves *reacting* to situations and events around us instead of properly *responding* to what we observe.

I understand the activity of *reacting* to be the process of skipping from Observe to Act in the OODA Loop. Before we give thought to the orientation, or take the time to effectively decide on the best action to take, we find ourselves reacting.

When we react to something without consideration, we are skipping from the Observe to the Act step of the loop. We may find ourselves doing this just to keep up with the stress and changes around us. We skip Orient and Decide because there is too much stimuli for our minds to process everything and to complete this cognitive process before we take action. With a lot on our plate, we may take comfort in this quick reaction to stimuli because we feel as though we are at least taking action, or "getting things done." If you have found yourself in this situation, or made a habit of reacting instead of completing an OODA Loop and responding to events in your life, you should have experience with the terrible consequences this can create.

When you merely react to a negative stimulus with a negative reaction, you only perpetuate negative energy. Through cause and effect, this will only bring more negative energy back to you. As this negative energy manifests, it will change your vibration and cause a downward spiral of negative actions.

When we can slow down the process of "dealing" with the world, we get to apply each step of the OODA Loop in proper form. By making it through each step of Observe, Orient, Decide and Act, we get to *respond* to situations and circumstances in our lives. In doing so, we allow our minds the time to orient, decide and act to negative stimuli. With the proper tools and a complete OODA loop, we are able to conjure a positive response to negative events, thus preventing the negative effect resulting from our actions.

Orient is the step where we get to apply our understanding of Universal Laws, namely Gender, Relativity, Polarity, Rhythm, and Cause and Effect, to properly gauge the nature of each event or stimulus that occurs. Once we observe an occurrence, we can use these Universal Laws to put the observation into perspective.

While Orienting, we can find the positive in each event or circumstance we observe, allowing us to identify more productive and positive options for responding. Once we get to the Decide step, we may use our understanding of Cause and Effect or Transmutation of Energy to determine the best action for responding to our particular circumstance. When we Act, we can do so with the thought of the Law of Vibration and be sure we find a way to perpetuate the positive energy, thus bringing back only more positive to us.

Imagine that a person walks into a room and begins yelling at you. This isn't something you anticipated, so you have no idea what caused the event or situation. If you were to *react* to this situation, you may Observe the yelling and then immediately Act to stop it or defend yourself. You skip the Orient and Decide steps and begin yelling back, deflecting the statements with contradictions and defenses.

From the outside looking in, you likely already know there is certainly no positive coming from this reaction. The argument will likely continue until someone storms away or decides to quit. Whatever caused the turmoil in the first place, and whatever the intended result of the confrontation was, it will be overshadowed by anger and frustration.

What if you could slow down this one event in your life and figure out how to *respond* instead of react? How would it look if you made it through the OODA Loop and dealt more constructively with this confrontation?

A friend enters the room and starts yelling. You *Observe* their anger and begin listening to their distress. This helps you *Orient* yourself to the situation, determining whether the issue is you, your actions or something else entirely—maybe they are upset about something at work or a breakup, and they are simply taking that frustration out on you. Once you have the information you need, you can *Decide* your best course of action: apologize, agree with them, or console them. And finally, you can *Act* to calm the situation with your selected response.

When you apply your understanding of the OODA Loop and allow yourself to complete the process by responding to events in your life, you do more than dispel a negative situation.

Every time you properly manage your spheres and choose to respond instead of react, you create a blueprint in your mind of how to effectively deal with a particular situation the next time.

The more you apply the tools you now have, the greater the mental database you will create of positive and effective responses that you can use when facing future problems. The longer you properly manage your Spheres, the easier and more effective this becomes.

Respecting Your Rhythm

T O MANAGE OUR SPHERES EFFECTIVELY, it is helpful to understand our body's natural rhythm. One consequence suggested by the Law of Rhythm is that our energy and state of being are in constant flux. We have times throughout the day, week and month that we feel especially energetic and positive, and we have times that we feel run down or unable to focus.

For me, I typically have a period of emotional letdown on Sunday evenings when I am preparing to go back to work. If I didn't rest much during the weekend, on Monday morning I tend to be a little sluggish in body and mind.

Tuesday through Thursday, I am quite energetic, focused and positive during the workday. In fact, this is usually when I get most of my work done for the week. By Friday afternoon, I am still ticking along, but my attention is easily distracted and by late afternoon—my mind has already left work, though my body remains.

I see this same rhythmic cycle during the day. When I wake up, I am sluggish for a few minutes. By the time I am finished getting ready for work, I am energetic and positive. After lunch, I am a little sluggish, but after dinner, I am energetic and positive once more.

It is important to understand your own energetic and emotional rhythm when managing your Spheres. When you understand your own rhythm, you can schedule your activities to benefit from your varying energy. We all make the best decisions and have the most effective OODA Loops when at these peaks.

When do you think it would be best to do some of the important things in your life, like managing your finances, making important life or career decisions, solving a problem at work, having a difficult conversation with a friend or working on a challenging project? Each of these things tends to require a substantial amount of focus and positive energy. If you aren't experiencing the results you would like with work, or are lacking your natural gusto when you tackle a difficult problem, consider the time of day or week you have been dealing with these issues. Was it at a time you were able to give your best effort?

Shouldn't we do everything when we are feeling at the top of our energetic and emotional peak? Well, maybe in an ideal world we could. But in this one, we have to deal with the Law of Rhythm and the fact that we will experience highs and lows in every aspect of life while still having to live that life. If we didn't do anything during the natural lows, we would lose a big piece of our days or weeks. There are plenty of things we can attend to when we aren't at our best. Doing a load of laundry or straightening up around the house doesn't require your best effort or highest emotional vibration. Running errands or exercising can be done when you don't have the emotional vibration to handle life challenges.

I mention this management of rhythm because our own frustrations or feelings of shortcomings can be a major source of negative energy in our Spheres. If we aren't getting the results from an activity that we feel we could, this can create dark clouds that loom. Part of managing your Direct Sphere is doing the best you can with what you have; we can achieve much greater results when we focus on the most important things in life at times when we are best suited to deal with them.

Understand, just because the Law of Rhythm is at work, this doesn't mean we are slaves to this natural cycle of emotional peaks and valleys. The Law of Rhythm will always influence us, but that doesn't mean we cannot experience or create a positive vibration during our rhythmic lows. Rhythm is just one of many factors that influence our emotional state.

When you are experiencing a time of rhythmic lull in emotional energy, there are many things you can do to overcome the darkness. Exercise is a great way to enliven yourself and find a natural boost in positive energy. Gratitude and giving to charity are two other tools we have already addressed that can create this same burst of positive emotional energy and vibration. Don't accept that you will be in a less positive vibration when the Law of Rhythm is working against you; just understand that this Law is at work and contributing to your total energy state, but it is just one factor that can be overcome.

Perception:
The Self-Fulfilling Prophecy

A S WE GO THROUGH LIFE, we formulate perceptions based on our observations and assumptions of the world around us. This is only natural—we all do it. But those perceptions can often turn into self-fulfilling prophecies.

The first time we meet someone, for instance, if they are rude or abrasive, we are left with the impression they are rude and abrasive by nature, and we think that this is just who they are. Sure, it's possible they have had a bad day, or that we inadvertently said something to offend them—but our perception is that they are rude. And should our paths cross with them again, we will likely approach them with that in mind, possibly being colder and more abrupt ourselves than we would normally be. This is sure to influence their behavior toward us as well.

These opinions and assumptions are often formed instinctively, which is why we place so much importance on the value of a first impression. First impressions can be hard to overcome. Once a person creates that perception of you in their mind (what kind of person you are and what you are capable of), they will treat you according to that perception.

But this also applies to how you experience the world. If you are constantly bracing yourself for the bad, you will invite that negative energy in. Heading into a first date with the perception that it is going to go poorly based solely on the assumptions you have made, almost definitely assures it will.

We create the nature of the Spheres we live in through our perceptions, and our perceptions are influenced by our assumptions. If I assume a movie, restaurant, or new boss is going to be bad, the chances are greater that I will create a perception that matches my assumption because our perceptions are always tinted by our assumptions.

When managing your Spheres, you can do a great deal to eradicate the dark clouds by just changing your assumptions. Assume tomorrow will be great and exciting. Tell yourself that the next person you meet will be awesome or your next meal at a restaurant will be fantastic. The change of assumption is the catalyst that will influence your observation and in turn, your perception.

> *As you think, so you are; as you imagine,*
> *so you become.*
>
> — UNKNOWN

Chapter 7

–––––––––––––––––– ◎ ––––––––––––––––––

Engaging with the World Around You

S O MUCH OF WHAT we have discussed up to now has involved the power of your own mind and how it relates to managing your spheres. But none of us is an island, and we are always contending with a world beyond our own thoughts. Understanding how to apply the Spheres to our interactions with those around us is the final step to achieving a happy and fulfilling life—and it is what the Action Sphere is all about.

Communication

Y OUR ABILITY TO AFFECT the world around you starts with communication. Don Miguel Ruiz, author of *The Four Agreements*, said it best when he acknowledged that communication is a double-edged sword. Through communication, we have the ability to create and spread all the positive energy we would care to contribute to the world, but we also have the opportunity to tear people down and spread all the hatred and discontent we can muster. It is the choice between spreading rays of sunshine or building dark clouds of hatred. Not everyone uses this power for good.

We have so much control over our environment and the life we experience. The energy we choose to put out is the energy we will get back; we are active participants in creating the environment around us, so the communication style we choose matters.

This spreads far beyond just the words we say. It also encompasses the actions we take that illustrate our thoughts, motives, intentions and character to others. Many times, our actions speak louder than our words.

> *Your actions speak so loudly, I cannot hear what you are saying.*
>
> — RALPH WALDO EMERSON

The nature of communication is different in each Sphere. Communication in the Indirect Sphere includes the news, gossip and rumors we hear. If it is a good story that you can get positive energy from, take it. If not, let it go.

Direct Sphere communication includes what people say to you or about you.

Communication in the Action Sphere includes everything you express to others, both in person and virtually. The ripples of how we communicate with others can extend far beyond us. Even a sour look or a comment made under your breath can create those ripples.

When dealing with communication in any Sphere, we can again apply the Universal Laws to find some positive nugget. For instance, the Law of Relativity would remind us that there could always be something worse than another person's words.

The Law of Rhythm applies to the health and energy of our friendships and relationships as well. We all experience low points with our friends and loved ones; this usually happens when negative communication occurs. Fortunately, when we get to these low points, we know that things will eventually get better as we rebound through rhythm.

Through the Law of Polarity, we are reminded that with every bad comes a good. When someone is communicating something negative to you, they are also communicating that you mean enough to them to spend that time and energy on you. You have such a significant role in their life that you have the power to affect them, and they have the willingness to commit the effort to discussing that with you. If we can sift through the painful emotions of the words they are saying, we can often find content that shares a message that will help us.

The other side of this coin is that when a particular friend only shares flattery and compliments, this too can have a negative impact. If we allow these thoughts to inflate our ego or feed our arrogance, even positive communication can have a negative result. And there is something to be said for friends who hold us accountable rather than being forever agreeable. We may have more to learn from those who are willing to help us see our own faults—as long as they speak from compassion and a desire to help and not from judgment.

Your words are your wand.
— FLORENCE SCOVILLE SCHINN

The Law of Transmutation of Energy speaks to conversations that inspire change, even from the disgust we may feel. Some conversations, even negative ones, can be the final straw, becoming the catalyst to ignite major life changes that will set the tide for a brighter future.

Considering the Law of Vibration, we must remember that our energy spreads to others. When someone communicates with enthusiasm and positive energy, those around them will begin to feel the same excitement. Look for environments where positive people mingle and get around them. Seek out positive friends and capture their energy.

There are certainly toxic situations and people who we would ultimately be better separating ourselves from. In those instances, if a harsh conversation is the catalyst to you making that move, the relief you will feel by removing that toxic influence from your life will be well worth the discomfort of one painful interaction. Make sure you are applying the OODA Loop prior to making that decision. In some cases, you may find that the person confronting you actually has a point to make—and by Observing and Orienting, you should be able to calmly approach the conversation and get to the root of the problem.

This same theory also applies to how you confront others. A calm and rational conversation will always accomplish more than one fueled by the heat of the moment. Take a step back and choose your words carefully. Remember, you can always escalate a conversation and the tone and frustration in your voice if the situation dictates. You cannot, however, explode in frustration at the beginning of a conversation and then back down and ever undo the harm you have caused. The display of anger and frustration will never be forgotten, even if it is forgiven.

Choose your words and tone carefully—how you communicate has the ability to send ripples far beyond what you might have assumed your reach to be.

Managing The Intruders

ONE OF THE GREAT THINGS about life is that we get to pick our friends and the people we spend our recreational time with. So, we can be choosy about those we commit that energy to, ensuring they are people who will uplift us and encourage us to be the best versions of ourselves. Unfortunately, there are also many coworkers, bosses and relatives that we would never have chosen to surround ourselves with, but we still have to associate with them. That's life.

We all know people who tend to bring us down. Maybe they always have something negative to say or some new drama they want to unload on us. Or perhaps they just have a way of getting under our skin, intruding into our otherwise peaceful state of mind.

I remember a time I was driving to pick up my daughter, planning to spend the night hanging out with her. When I pulled up to her daycare, I noticed an email notification had just come through on my phone. Seeing the sender's name, I was very curious about what the email might say, but I was hesitant to read it. Based on my previous experiences with this person, I knew it was likely going to be something negative—either an issue I would have to deal with or some bit of information that didn't directly pertain to me, but might likely alter my mood, nonetheless.

I also knew that I was about to spend time with my daughter, which meant that even if this email was about something that would require my attention, I couldn't deal with it now. So, instead of reading the email and taking on the possible negative vibration or mental distraction it likely held, I chose to ignore it until I was in a better place to deal with the issue or bad news it might bring.

I pushed the email (a potential intruder to my positive vibration) aside until I was prepared to deal with it—knowing that right now, just as I was about to pick up my daughter, was not that time.

It can be hard to resist the temptation to let yourself down from the high of being productive and available all the time. It feels great to be needed, to indulge in every opportunity to solve a problem or correct a mistake. In fact, that drive has created a culture that has us all believing we should be forever connected. It's why so many of us struggle to transition from "work time" to "personal time." But when you can make the choice to establish a time and place for those intruders, any mental distraction whether positive or negative, you are doing a much better job of protecting your own vibration.

The bubble we live our lives in is a precious space. The energy in that bubble is the energy within us and vice versa. Part of managing our spheres is effectively managing that energy in our bubble by controlling when and how much negative energy we let into our personal space—both mental and physical.

We all have to deal with negative people, events and circumstances from time to time. That is just a part of life. But none of us needs to be connected around the clock, inviting those intruders in at all hours. When we make ourselves available is a choice. Like that email I refused to read, we can often block things from entering our sphere when we aren't in the right vibration to handle them.

But you have to be willing to prioritize your own mental wellbeing first.

It's Not A Selfish Thing

I MENTIONED SKIPPING A PHONE CALL or possibly ignoring someone to protect your vibration. That may seem like a particularly selfish thing to do—to ignore someone. And perhaps protecting your vibration rather than connecting with someone who is reaching out to you is a little selfish. But it is selfless as well.

If you are choosing not to connect with someone because you are not in a positive vibration, you are protecting them from being negatively affected by you when you are not able to give your best. You are protecting them from any negative energy you may emit.

Have you ever run into an old friend and known the second they spoke that they were in a funk? It probably left you with a feeling that you wished you hadn't run into them at that moment. Saving others from that experience by skipping a phone call or waiting to respond isn't merely a selfish act. You are also protecting yourself and others by not engaging when you aren't a more positive version of yourself. If you didn't care what negative energy you might emit, or lack of care you might express, what does that say about how you see or respect the other person?

Ride The Wave

THE NEXT PIECE OF "managing your vibration" is managing when you choose to tackle various things that may eat away at your positive vibration or put you into a negative vibration. When you have an important event or special time approaching, should you expose yourself to something that may affect your vibration just before that event? Like the email I chose to ignore before picking up my daughter, I was making the decision to not allow my vibration to take a hit before I began an evening that I wanted to be particularly enjoyable.

It would be great to live in a world where nothing existed that put us into a negative vibration. Unfortunately, even with perfect management of your Spheres, you can't hope to live the rest of your life with no experience or event that detracts from your positive vibration. Of course, you shouldn't want to either. It is during the hard times that we grow. It is the struggles and negative vibration creating experiences that give us the ammunition to appreciate the good in life. Just as tilling the soil in a field prepares it for an abundant yield of crops, the struggles that tear down our vibration and challenge our character are what prepare our mind and soul for the abundance of joy and prosperity that we can enjoy.

Sometimes, these challenging things are foreseeable or predictable. There are some things I must do, like chores around the house, which I don't particularly enjoy and which take a toll on my vibration. There are acquaintances I must work with or speak to that don't bode particularly well for my vibration. After a financially challenging week or month, paying the bills may not leave me in the greatest vibration.

These are all examples of things I can foresee or predict that will take a toll on my emotional state. If I become aware of the resultant vibration these activities may leave, I can avoid attending to them before a period of time I want especially to enjoy.

Have you ever had an argument with a friend or a challenging episode at work that you carried in your mind during a date or special celebration? Have you ever raced to finish some chore or activity you were excited to do just before you planned to relax or enjoy some time off? Part of managing your Spheres is being aware of what puts you in a negative vibration and avoiding these things at times you are not best suited to deal with to deal with them.

Imagine you experience a rhythm of emotional energy as I do, which leaves you feeling particularly drained at the end of each week. Say you are on your way home from work on Friday, not in a particularly good vibrational state, and you take a phone call from a relative or old friend that you aren't usually excited to speak with. After 10 minutes or so of chatting with this person, your worn emotional vibration has taken another hit from the conversation and left you in a mood that is not particularly fun to be around.

When you get home, you rush to get ready for a date night with your significant other. The stress of rushing to get ready takes another toll on your vibration. Now think, what version of yourself are you bringing to an evening that should be a special time? Are you presenting the best version of yourself? A version that should exhibit the gratitude and appreciation you would want to during such an event?

What if this were a new romantic interest or a special celebration with your friends? Are you setting yourself up well for this evening or could you have done better to help it be what you would want and to give the best of yourself to your company?

The answer is, of course you haven't set yourself up for an enjoyable evening, and you haven't prepared yourself to be the best company to be around, either.

So, what could you do instead? Maybe plan to make your date later in the evening so you don't have to rush. Or skip the phone call from the person who regularly takes a toll on your vibration.

The mere fact of acknowledging the upcoming evening could give you an opportunity to apply the Universal Laws to any stressors in your life and put yourself in a positive vibration before the evening even begins. Taking a moment to assess your vibration and identify anything that may be affecting it may be all you need to do to prevent yourself from falling into a funk or being in a position where you exhibit less than your best.

Better than just avoiding things that could put you into a negative vibe, you can take a more proactive approach and purposely do something that puts you into a positive vibration. Maybe there is something you know works for you, like meditating, yoga, reading a book, or taking a walk. How much better could many experiences in your life be if you purposely put yourself into a particularly positive vibration before those events began?

Patience

S O, WHAT SHOULD YOU DO when those intruders are unavoidable and you find yourself face to face with a person or situation that has the ability to bring you down?

Well, that is when I would argue that a little patience can go a long way.

For most of my life, I have tended to be a very patient person. Over the past few years, I have further developed this tendency by trying to appreciate and understand the history and motives behind people's actions. When I experience someone who is enraged or acting selfishly, I try to imagine a reason for their behavior. I attempt to step back and piece together in my mind a story about the person's history, an experience they may have had that is contributing to their mood or a circumstance they are currently under that is fueling the way they are acting.

Being a father has given me a wonderful opportunity to consider and develop this kind of analysis. This role has given me the chance to practice looking for these causes of behavior and piecing together contributing factors through my engagement with my daughter.

If you have ever spent time with a toddler, you understand the wide range of moods and reactions they may exhibit in any given day. Dealing with these mood swings and behavior changes has provided a great opportunity to develop my habit of seeing things through another's eyes. It is much easier to figure out why a four-year-old may be acting a certain way or having a meltdown than it is to understand the emotional meltdowns of a thirty-year-old, but the same idea applies.

My daughter is typically very well behaved and attentive to all that is going on around her. She listens and communicates very well for her age. She is considerate and adorable at the same time, all while being the silliest person I know. (I may be a little biased, but... I'm her dad, I'm entitled.)

When my daughter isn't listening to what I say or isn't paying particular attention to what is going on around her, I know there must be a reason for this abnormal behavior. When her mood fluctuates, I can usually trace it back to a cause.

A lack of attention or carelessness typically occurs when she is very excited about something. I see this when a grandparent has just come to town or when we have big plans coming up. The excitement causes her mood to change and becomes a contributing factor to her loss of attention.

Similarly, there are times when she is cranky, whiney, or seems to be sad. This occurs most often on days when she is tired, has missed a nap or, on occasion, when she is coming down from a sugar high.

I believe I understand the moods of my four-year-old daughter fairly well, to the point where I can often predict the changes before they occur. This helps significantly with my own peace of mind. When I predict a mood swing or a tantrum, it is much easier to deal with. When I can trace her behavior back to a cause, the greatest benefit is how much easier it becomes to accept and deal with the behavior or actions she is exhibiting.

For instance, when my daughter begins whining about something and it starts to irritate me, I tie the mood back to factors that may have caused it. Maybe I was busy all day and my errands prevented her from taking a nap, thus causing her to be tired and cranky. Or maybe her lack of attention can be attributed to the excitement she is feeling because Nana just came to town. When I piece this together, I am able to gain better control of my own patience with her.

I, too, have been overly excited at times in my life. I, too, have been exhausted and allowed it to affect my mood and actions. How could I justify getting frustrated with a four-year-old for doing the same thing?

A preschooler only has so much life experience and usually only a handful of factors contribute to the way they are acting. As we grow older and gain life experience, the factors contributing to our mood and behavior become exponentially more complex.

What is simple with a four-year-old can be much more difficult with a thirty-year-old, and even more so with a stranger. Still, it helps to remember that everyone always has a story of their own. We have no idea what a person has experienced in their day, week or life that is contributing to their actions.

To keep my patience with others, I have found I don't actually need to understand the *exact* reason a person is acting as they are. As long as I can imagine *a* reason, it makes the experience much easier to digest. Sometimes, it helps to remember times from my own life when I haven't been at my best, and to recall the reasons. A little introspection can do wonders for helping us to have patience with others, remembering the times when it would have been nice for someone else to have a little patience with us.

> *Be kind, for everyone you meet is fighting a battle*
> *you know nothing about.*
>
> — WENDY MASS

Choosing Your Friends

I T ISN'T ALWAYS OTHERS who are struggling or are in the wrong. There are times when we all find ourselves in a position where we cannot see the best action to take. Or worse, we can't think of any action to take at all. With most things in life, we can't do anything to achieve the best possible outcome when we work at it alone.

Living your life in a positive and productive way is no different. There will be times when you are in a rut and won't be able to find your way out. Don't be afraid to ask for help from another person. Share your pain and frustration with a friend who may be able to provide a different perspective on your situation. It is often easier to see the solutions to a set of circumstances when we aren't distracted by the pain and frustration of being in the middle of them.

We have all experienced a situation where a friend was in a bad way, and we could easily see the solution to their problems that they just weren't finding for themselves. When we get stuck in the reaction loop of O-A, we may need a hand to ground us back to an effective OODA Loop.

I caution, however, that you pick the right kind of friend when you are in need. Be sure the person you reach out to is standing on higher ground than you at the time. We all likely have someone we can turn to that may help us justify our pain and just perpetuate a bad situation. Maybe this is the best help they know to give, or they meet us in a funk because they are in a similar state themselves. As they say, misery loves company, but this kind of friendship isn't they kind you need when facing the most challenging of times.

What you need in these situations is a friend who is going to help pull you out, not one who is going to only pull you along, or worse, pull you down further.

I once heard a parable that illustrates the epitome of great friendship:

> A guy is walking down the street one day when he trips and falls into a hole. The hole is deep and the walls are steep, leaving this guy no way out.
>
> After many hours, a doctor walked past the hole, so the guy shouts for help. "Hey, Doc! Can you help me out of this hole?" Not sure how he can help, the doctor writes a prescription, throws it in the hole and moves on.
>
> A few hours later, a priest walks by and the guy shouts up, "Father, I'm down in a hole; can you please help me out?" Not sure what else to do, the priest decides to pray with the man down in the hole and then moves on.

Then a friend walks by, and the guy shouts, "Hey, friend, it's me. I am stuck in this hole; can you help me out?" The friend jumps in the hole and stands beside him. "Are you stupid? Now we're both stuck down here!!"

The friend says, "Yeah, but I've been down here before. And, I know the way out."

We all need friends like this ... friends who recognize they have been there before, are willing to get dirty with us, as long as the goal is finding the light together.

Focus on finding the right kind of friends, those who encourage you to always be the best version of yourself, and all the rest will seem so much easier to embrace. If you have that sort of friend in your life already, be sure they are the one you turn to in time of need.

Section Three

────────── ◎ ──────────

Bite-Size Recap

O NE OF THE THINGS I hope you will take away from this section is an understanding of just how much control you really have over the world in which you live.

Imagine a leaf blown from a tree in the park. As the leaf falls toward the ground, it flutters back and forth under the influence of any breeze or wind it encounters. The unchangeable shape of the leaf predetermines the way the wind will catch and blow it as it falls to the ground. The leaf's final destination on the earth is determined by the whims of the breeze that day. It cannot control its direction, nor does it have any specific place it wishes to fall.

Compare this rigid leaf to the wings of a butterfly. As a butterfly flaps its wings, it has the ability to determine and fly toward a destination. Both a leaf and a butterfly are influenced by any breeze that may come along, but the butterfly is in control. A breeze can influence the flight path of the butterfly; a strong wind could blow it around beyond the butterfly's flight ability. But the butterfly can still flap its wings and influence its path. Eventually, the wind will subside, and the butterfly will once again progress toward its desired location.

When I compare the leaf and the butterfly, it makes me think of the power of having a conscious and positive mental attitude. If you were unaware of your thoughts or ability to affect them, your path through life is much like the leaf falling to the ground. Your thoughts are at the whim of the world going on around you. You are influenced by the negativity you see; challenges and obstacles placed before you will stop or alter your path. When you are unaware of your power to control your own thoughts, you fall through life like a leaf falling to the ground. You are pushed in each and every direction that the winds blow you. Your mind, attitude and actions are influenced by the environment and energy of others.

Once we enlighten ourselves to the power of our mental attitude, and learn some tools to increase our own positive energy, we allow our bodies and minds to take flight like the butterfly. We are still influenced by our environment and life events, just as the butterfly is influenced by the breeze. But the butterfly has wings of his own, and tools to influence his direction, regardless of the direction and magnitude of the wind. Like a butterfly flapping its wings, with the right mental awareness and tools, we can steer ourselves in the direction of our goals and dreams. We don't travel through life at the whim of outside forces; we control the direction we move. When a butterfly hits the ground, it can take flight again. If blown by a strong wind, or pushed off course by an opposing breeze, the butterfly can prevail and still find its way back to the destination it desires.

A positive mental attitude and a mastery of any philosophy we discuss won't prevent hardship or rid your life of challenges. We will all face hard and difficult challenges, but we can each prevail against the whims of the outside world. We each have control to overcome challenges and fly our way to a better tomorrow.

Don't worry if you have been messing up some of these ideas in your own life. What I have presented in this book is likely a wide departure from the way you have understood and lived your life thus far. If you choose to implement some of these new perspectives into your own life now, it will take time and energy to adjust to a new way of thinking. You will have to develop new habits and emotional responses to replace the old ones.

I have personally spent much of my life working against these Laws, mismanaging my Spheres and dealing with the anguish and frustration that such living creates. Even as I aspire to master these ideas in my own life, I too occasionally slip up and become victim to my old ways of thinking.

I eventually recognize the positive, or I identify my wasted energy from dealing with frustrations, and I am able to get back to amplifying my positive vibration in order to return to the happy state we all aspire to. With every opportunity to practice, I become better. With more experience, I spend much less time in the negative realm, and the positive emotions I experience are amplified far beyond anything I previously knew to be possible. The same can be true for you, as well.

> **Contributors to Cloudy Skies:** The news, negative television, interactions with others and the past. Remember how to differentiate between what is Indirect and Direct (does this directly affect you and do you have to respond?). Find ways to move past those cloudy skies in the Indirect Sphere. Using the Laws can help.

OODA Loop Steps

- **Observe** the situation. This occurs naturally and consistently. When something has you bothered, acknowledge it.
- **Orient** yourself to whatever that is. Is it in your Indirect Sphere or Direct Sphere? If it is in the Indirect Sphere,

evaluate whether it is positive or negative. If it is negative, let it go! If the event occurs in your Direct Sphere, can you use the Universal Laws to see it in a positive way?

- o **Decide** what UL will help you find the positive or what action you should take. If there is no way to find the positive, what can you do to prevent the event from occurring again or to remove yourself from the circumstance?

- o **Act** in order to change your future result.

Before you allow other persons' behavior or actions to create a dark cloud in your sky, remember that everyone has their own story and reasons for their behavior. Exhibit patience and kindness, and never forget that communication is one of the biggest tools you have in your Action Sphere—use it wisely.

Section Three

◎

Applying What You've Learned

Dark Clouds In The News

W E DISCUSSED HOW the news can contribute to dark clouds in your sky, but I'm not sure people realize just how negative the news really is—so I have an experiment I want you to complete.

Keep a piece of paper with you the next time you decide to catch up with what's happening in the world. As you watch or read the news, tally all the negative stories against all of the positive ones. If it has to do with a crime being committed, a story of financial despair, a pending economic crisis, mass layoffs, or drama in some celebrity's life, mark it down as a negative story. These are negative because they will only bring negative thoughts and emotions to your mind when you hear them.

From my experience, three negative stories for every positive one is a fairly good ratio. More often, I witness five negative stories to every positive. There have even been days when the ratio I have experienced was ten to one. If a major story has just broken, like a train derailment or a factory explosion, you will be hard pressed to find any positive news stories sprinkled into the news cycle.

But every negative story doesn't necessarily *have* to bring a dark cloud to your sky, does it? Well... that's Part II of this experiment.

As you watch and tally the negative stories, try to use the Law of Polarity or Relativity to look for the positive in every story. After all, that's what the Laws are all about, right?

You will find that while it is certainly possible to put a positive spin on the stories you see, the task becomes exhausting fast due to the speed with which negative news stories are fed to us. It takes a conscious effort to listen to every news story and find the positive. We often play the news in the background or as we zone out relaxing on the couch. If we aren't actively looking for the positive, all those negative messages, and the energy they create, penetrate straight to our conscious and subconscious mind.

But don't just take my word for it. Do the experiment for yourself, perhaps over a few days. Then, review your tallies and ask yourself, "Is watching or reading the news really worth bringing all those dark clouds into your sky?"

Tactical Mission:
The OODA Loop At Play

THIS IS A FUN EXPERIMENT that simply requires you to have a partner to play with. Hint: For those of you with kids, this can be a great bonding activity!

We discussed how the OODA Loop comes in handy during sporting events and military missions, but I want you to practice mastering your own OODA Loop and disrupting that of your opponent on a smaller scale, for instance, during a game of checkers with your child or a hand of poker with your friend or spouse.

Throughout the course of the game, consciously practice the OODA Loop as you make your moves. For example, if you're playing Battleship with your niece or nephew:

1. Observe the board, analyzing the hits and misses you have already made

2. Orient yourself based on those hits and misses, determining where the possible ship configurations reside.

3. Decide what your best move may be, likely opting for a location that would eliminate the most possible configurations.

4. Act by calling your number out.

Pay attention to how your OODA Loop resets with each and every new move.

As you master this, look for ways to disrupt your opponent's OODA Loop. If playing video games with a friend, try some distraction tactics or change your own moves up so quickly that they don't have a chance to process. Witness the frustration that takes place, and the rash decisions that are made when the OODA Loop is interrupted—and try to relate this back to times when you haven't been able to process through your own OODA Loop.

Depending on with whom you are playing, the reaction may be humorous—but don't let this game go too far into the realm of creating dark clouds in someone else's sky. Particularly if you are playing with a child, let them in on your game sooner rather than later and then practice going through and disrupting the OODA Loop together!

Bonus Challenge: Look for examples of interrupted OODA Loops in some of your favorite books, movies and television shows. The more aware you become of these instances, the more likely you will be able to avoid them in your own life. You will find that many fiction plots actually use a disrupted OODA Loop, or an abrupt move from Observe to Act, in order to serve as a catalyst for the drama. Turn to the Exercise Appendix at the back of this book for a few examples.

Section Four:
The Final Pieces

The Big Things

───────────── ◎ ─────────────

M ANY OF THE EXAMPLES presented in this book may seem quite trivial when compared to a major life event. The death of a loved one, an unexpected pregnancy, learning you have a terminal illness, or even the sudden loss of a job (threatening to make you and your family homeless); these are major life events that will likely knock you down so much harder than a traffic jam or your computer refusing to cooperate.

Unfortunately, the hardships and heartache that come from major tragedies won't be neatly or easily remedied by applying the Universal Laws or pondering your Spheres. It is sometimes impossible to protect yourself from major challenges in life, and there is no quick and easy way to snap your fingers and make tragedy disappear. But the principles in this book will always make it easier to weather the storm.

Managing your Spheres is the mental conditioning that will make every day better, giving you the preparation necessary to handle the major life challenges should they arise. If you are knocked to the ground by the loss of a close friend or pending divorce, established habits of managing your Spheres will enable you to deal more easily with the trivial things that arise in the midst of a major event. A rainy day, some bad traffic or a flat tire will still occur, but they won't suffocate you or provide that final straw if you are adept at handling such things in stride.

To put it in a different context, eating healthy and exercising regularly won't necessarily keep you from getting cancer, but having a healthy and strong body will improve your chances, and make treatment much easier to endure, should you face such a traumatic diagnosis. Managing your Spheres every day is the healthy diet and exercise that will make the tragedies more surmountable; it won't prevent or cure every problem you might face, but it will strengthen your reserves so that you are better equipped to deal with whatever comes your way.

Learn, apply, and master managing your Spheres when things in your life are not tragically awry so that you can have the strength to tackle those hurdles when they do appear.

The Choice Of Happiness

———————————◎———————————

ONE CONSEQUENCE YOU WILL discover from managing your Spheres is the ability to find and harness the happiness that comes from within. It starts by looking for the opportunity that comes from your struggles. Look for the lessons you learned from your mistakes, and take solace in the knowledge and experience you can then take with you into the future. Don't let the things beyond your control affect you.

Russell Conwell was an inspirational speaker, writer, minister, philanthropist and lawyer. He also served as the first President of Temple University from 1887 to 1925, where he once delivered a speech that would carry on long after his death. Titled "Acres of Diamonds,[2]" Conwell used this speech to tell the moving story of a man who went out in search of what he desired. The story is centered on Al Hafed, who owned a successful farm and had a happy family.

One day Al Hafed learned that diamonds were a magical gem, capable of bringing him great wealth, fortune and all the happiness he could enjoy. He heard that these diamonds could be

---

2   "Acres of Diamonds", Russel Conwell. To download the complete story, visit http://www.temple.edu/about/history/acres-diamonds

found in white sand riverbeds all around Africa and that anyone who wanted to could go out and collect a diamond for himself.

Hafed sold his farm, made arrangements for his family to live elsewhere, and set off to find himself some diamonds. After many months of travel, he was tired, hungry and destitute. What's worse, he had found no diamonds. He had traveled all over Africa and into Europe looking, but had produced little more than disappointment, frustration and despair. Penniless and tired, having reached the end of his rope, Hafed ended his journey by jumping from a high cliff into the ocean below.

While he was on this journey, other actions were transpiring back home. The gentleman who bought Al Hafed's farm spent his days tending to it. Occasionally, this man would walk with his kids down to a stream that cut through the land. One afternoon, he saw an interesting rock lying in the sand by the stream. It was mostly dark gray and black in color, but it had a beautiful quartz stone inside that was shining through. Thinking nothing of it, the new farmer took the rock home and placed it on his mantel. A few weeks later, this farmer had a visitor who noticed the rock and let out a gasp.

The rock was not just some quartz; it was one of the largest diamonds ever found. After further inspection, it was discovered that there were many acres of diamonds littered all over the farmland Hafed had once owned.

Al Hafed had gone out searching for something he had right on his own farm the whole time.

The inspiration found in this story does not come from the tragedy that Hafed suffered in his quest. It comes from the understanding that Al Hafed lost his way only when he got it into his mind that he had to go out and find his happiness rather than seeking it from within.

For many of us, happiness and fulfillment in life is our special diamond. We go out into the world looking for a source of that happiness. Unfortunately, what we find is disappointment in ourselves and the world around us when that happiness isn't easily found. We become convinced we have been robbed of it. We search through books, take classes, ask friends and travel the world looking for a source of happiness to replenish whatever it is we are sure we are lacking.

If we could just stop for a moment and reflect, we would see that we have everything we need to be happy right within us. You already have everything you need to be as happy and satisfied with your life as you could possibly hope to be. That does not mean you should stop striving for your dreams, or working toward some new goal, but it does mean that you should stop waiting for tomorrow to be happy. You don't have to reach the next step to find the happiness that you are already completely capable of experiencing.

There is no substance, secret or skill you have to discover to make yourself fulfilled. Stop looking outside of yourself for the contentment only you can produce. Until you can make the choice to look within as a means of harvesting the greatest diamonds of all, you will never discover the source of happiness you have been searching for all along.

With the ideas I am sharing, I am proposing a shift in the way you view and interact with the Universe. This will require a small change for some and a drastic course correction for others. I expect any idea you pick up from this book can bring a positive change in your life. But it is important to know that simply being aware of the ideas presented in this book won't bring automatic results; to get the most benefit, you must work at it.

I often find my mind taking a first step in the wrong direction when I am faced with a challenge or frustration. I was conditioned to think in a certain way for many years of my life, so it is only natural that I (and you) may still struggle at times. What I have found is the more I practice and the more exposure I have with these new ways of thinking and managing my life, the easier it becomes.

Take some notes as you experience life, and refer to them often to identify where you might improve for tomorrow. Keep at it and invest that energy; the reward is more than worth it!!

Call To Action

———————◎———————

THROUGHOUT OUR LIFE EXPERIENCES, many of us have been conditioned to give up control in some way. We can see that life is a series of ups and downs. At times, with small struggles, we may feel it is best to just relinquish the reigns and accept our fate. I want you to challenge that way of thinking and to recognize what I am so thankful to have learned myself: we have far more control over the events and outcomes in our life than most of us realize. You are in a position to create your own destiny, to make your own happiness and orchestrate the life you want to lead. It starts with understanding how to gain that control in the first place.

My goal for you is to raise the awareness of Sphere segregation, and more constructively deal with the things in life that we all must. In this way, you will find yourself empowered to manage your Spheres. By reducing the amount of "stuff" that affects your emotional vibration, you shrink the size of your Direct Sphere. You may then search for the positive in everything that remains, and to make the best of your Action Sphere to create the world around you as you desire it to be.

When I discuss shrinking your Direct Sphere, I merely mean that you are shrinking the perceived size of it. You are recognizing all the things in life that seem to have a direct effect on you, but shouldn't. You realize that much of the news can't affect you. You understand that a grudge someone holds against you or an action from your own past can only affect you if you let it. You recognize how insignificant these things actually are to your day-to-day happiness and then you refuse to give them any more of your energy, thus shrinking the Sphere.

In order to shrink your Direct Sphere, you identify the many things that commandeer your emotions or distract your attention, you find the Indirect Sphere events and circumstances that are having a direct effect on you, and you push them back to the Indirect Sphere where they belong. Then, you deal with the many things that remain in your Direct Sphere to find the positive from those events and circumstances. You examine each tragedy, struggle, or challenge to find the benefit or positive advantage it brings to your life. If you can't find a positive no matter how you examine something in your life, then you think of something that could have been much worse. In this last ditch effort, you can at least be grateful that things aren't as bad as they could be. This will give you a little something positive to focus on while you weather the storm.

When even this technique fails to ease the burden of some event or situation, try to instead focus on the things in your life that are going well. What do you still have to be grateful for? No matter how large, dark and scary a particular rain cloud may be, there is still beauty to be found if you look away.

The first two Spheres comprise everything that comes into our lives. The Action Sphere represents all the energy we emit. We may have once believed that our actions unto the world and the energy we receive from the world were two isolated things. This is not the case. The energy we emit to the environment around us has a direct influence on the energy we receive from the world.

The only way to minimize the number of new dark clouds coming into our lives is to stop emitting poisonous energy. Manage your Spheres to find the sunshine; be that person who is that ray of sunshine for others.

Imagine for a moment two different friends or relatives in your life. One is always a grump. He seems to find the negative in everything he sees. He can spot the hole in all of your accomplishments and the downfall behind all the good news he hears.

Your other friend is grateful and happy all of the time. When you share stories of your life, she can appreciate the good in every accomplishment and help you find the benefit that may come from any challenge. This second friend is elated anytime she sees you and is grateful for your friendship. Any gift or souvenir you share with this positive friend, no matter how small or insignificant, is received with great excitement and appreciation.

Now ask yourself, who are you more likely to share your blessings with? If you came into great fortune and had some abundance to share, if you won a few tickets to an all-expenses-paid vacation or a gift certificate to a new restaurant and could only take one friend, whom would you choose?

The Universe is no different with the blessings it shares with us.

"Post hoc ergo proctor hoc" is a Latin phrase that translates to "after, therefore, because." We often perceive life with this fallacy when we believe that people are happy and successful because of events that have come to them previously in their own lives. The rationale is that someone is cheerful and positive because they have been blessed and lucky in their life.

The Universal Laws would suggest this is not the case. The Laws of Cause and Effect and Vibration suggest that we attract blessings and good fortune to us, before the signs of exuberant happiness come. People with the greatest blessings and luck in their life aren't happy because of these positive events. They attract these positive things to their life because they were happy, grateful and positive people before the blessings arrived. This is what we mean and feel when we suggest someone "got what was coming to them." When a kind-hearted and selfless person wins a promotion or catches a lucky break, we say they got what they deserved. Similarly, when a nasty or rude person is struck with misfortune or a tough break, they don't become a grump because of that experience. We know they were a nasty person before that bad luck arrived.

If you are holding back on your happiness and positive charm to shine until the moment your ship roles in, think again. Your gratitude and kindness must precede your great success, not the other way around. Remember Lincoln's, "When I do good, I feel good. When I do bad, I feel bad." The good action—thoughts, words or deeds—comes *before* the good feeling.

I want you to stop emitting negative energy into the environment. When we live in an environment where our Direct Sphere is loaded with negative energy, one of the biggest steps we can take to clear the air is to cut off the flow of negative energy we are putting out there. When that negative energy emission is stopped, you can work on growing your Sphere of Action as large as possible.

I presented the Action Sphere at first as being the smallest of the three because I think it is easiest to visualize it that way. But really, the size of your Action Sphere is independent of your Direct and Indirect Spheres. It can be as large or small as you want to make it.

Think of how big the Action Sphere is of a person who has few friends and makes little contact with the rest of the world.

Compare that to the Action Sphere of an author, a public speaker or someone who uses their life to change the lives of others. When you share a positive message, try to make your Action Sphere as large as possible. If you are a source of positive energy and your voice and actions make the environment around you better for your involvement, why not make that sphere reach as far as possible?

The promise of this book is to help you create the life you desire; this comes by the repeated application of tools to managing your Spheres. While it is sometimes cliché, the statement that our perception is our reality is honest. The way we perceive our lives is, in fact, the way we experience life. When we perceive negative things around us, our life is negative. The reality we feel is directly tied to this perception. When we have a great day, the perception that everything in life is great attracts to our attention other evidence that this feeling is true. We influence our perception by the thoughts in our mind. And the vibration we hold within influences the observations that develop our perception.

We create the life we desire by making what we desire our new reality. If you are unhappy with your circumstances, change them. Take different actions or create new habits, allowing you to create a different reality. Do not underestimate the magnitude of that which you can control. Even when you cannot change your external circumstances, you can change the way the events around you affect you and how you respond to them.

.

Statement Of Hope

—————————— ◎ ——————————

For things in your life to change,
you have to change.

— JIM ROHN

I F YOU WANT THE RESULTS you are getting in life to change, or you want the feelings of happiness and satisfaction to improve, then you have to change how you relate to the world. Only by changing the way that you relate with the Direct and Indirect Spheres, and by changing the way you emit energy through your Sphere of Action, will you be able to change the results you are getting and find the peace of mind and abundance of happiness that you would like to enjoy.

At first, it may seem overwhelming to have to take such action and make so many changes to yourself. But this is the most exciting and empowering part! You don't have to change the world out there for your *experience* to change drastically. You don't have to change how your friends act or people treat you. You don't have to change the weather or the economy, and you don't have to change the price of oil or the members of congress in order to get different results from life.

The only thing you have to change is you. I am not saying you have to change the person you are at the core; you don't need to change your likes, dislikes, skills, talents or passions. You don't need to change your DNA, your name, your family or your job. The only thing you have to change is one relationship: the relationship you have with the world around you.

Yes, this will take some practice. It will take hard work for a while, before it gets easy. But eventually, it will become natural. If you make the effort now, what seems a little challenging at first *will* one day become second nature. Committing to a change today means seeing things in a different way and allowing the rest of your life to change forever as well. It won't be instantaneous; it won't happen overnight. But it will happen.

You fell down more than just a few times when you learned to walk. You were slow the first time you tried to read. Riding a bike was probably difficult at first. But now you have the mastery of each of these skills, and your life is better for it. The benefit of gaining a few habits to change the way you relate with the world can be just as significant. Anything worth doing takes a little time and energy, but soon it will be second nature, and the benefits will last forever.

Aren't you ready for a change?

Epilogue

———————— ◎ ————————

I WAS IN A BAD PLACE, both personally and professionally, when I deployed to Afghanistan a few years ago. I felt as though I lacked balance in every area of my life. Work obligations kept me physically and emotionally overloaded, which frustrated things in my personal life. Issues in my personal life weighed on me while at work, which restrained my professional aspirations. I realized my life had been marching down a road toward a future that I no longer desired. Even worse, I wasn't exactly sure where that road was heading.

Obligations in most areas of my life conflicted with my interests in others. I poured myself into my work at the cost of managing my health and relationships. I neglected my fitness and the pursuit of my hobbies and passions, thereby restricting my own sense of self. I worked very hard at everything on my plate and was doing the best I felt I could to live and manage a fulfilling and happy life—though I felt anything but fulfilled or happy.

To an onlooker, I may have appeared to enjoy a great life with many things going well. But from my point of view, there was something significant lacking. For as hard as I was working, and as exhausted as I was by the effort, I should have felt more fulfilled and joyful. I expected a greater payout for all the exertion I was a putting in—more happiness, fulfillment and sense of purpose.

I wanted to know whether the road I was traveling could lead me to fulfilling my true passions and desires. When I left for deployment, I drew a line in the sand. I was determined to figure out how to fill the emotional void I felt within. I needed new direction, a few new ideas and the answers to the questions that had long puzzled me about the nature of life, happiness, and finding fulfillment and purpose in the world.

My deployment offered me the perfect opportunity to reflect, ponder, learn and find some answers. Having just achieved a major professional accomplishment I had pursued for nearly five years, I now had the chance to focus my attention on something other than climbing that ladder.

I also found myself in an interesting position concerning my personal life. A deployment removes you from most of the people, things and activities you know. I gained reprieve from my normal life experience and was offered an opportunity to reflect on that existence from the sideline.

For the next six months, I was dedicated to reading as many books as I could get my hands on, searching for new ideas and possible solutions. I read biographies and self-help books, I watched recorded seminars about personal growth and happiness, and I listened to sermons from various religions. I paid closer attention to the ideas discussed around me, wondering if maybe someone else was sharing a solution to a struggle I faced. Before long, I began to notice a few common themes, or core truths, that emerged from all the various resources I had exposed myself to.

There seemed to be some apparent truths about the world that shared a common thread in the ideas and philosophies I was learning. I gathered pieces to the puzzle from multiple disciplines, but I never found one source that clearly articulated the ideas that were developing in my mind.

My introduction to the Universal Laws finally began to clarify these ideas. I discovered a common fabric between the concepts shared in the many books and lectures I was exposing myself to. My search was heading in the right direction. My evolving awareness of these Laws provided a new vocabulary that allowed me to more fully understand the various ideas I kept coming across. The Universal Laws provided a framework for understanding everything more clearly.

I began to realize that I had been learning about these concepts, in some form or another, for many years. These simple and precise Universal Laws helped to unlock the solution to many of the mysteries I had long pondered, from relationships and happiness, to professional success and personal achievement.

What amazed me the most about my discovery of these Universal Laws was that once I understood the vocabulary and context, I was able to find evidence of them being described everywhere. I began to identify these core principles at the heart of everything else I have since learned. Once I was introduced to the Universal Laws, I underwent a major philosophical change in my life. For the first time, I was able to make sense of some of the issues I had pondered for years.

Within the context of the Universal Laws, I began to understand why certain circumstances occurred the way they had in my life. I could pinpoint where much of the frustration I experienced had originated. But, most importantly, I had new hope that I could take control of my thoughts, emotions and actions in a way that would allow me to create any future I desired. Our understanding of the world that exists around us, as well as the source of our hopes and ambitions for the future, will always evolve over the years. But for the first time, I recognized the nature of my ambitions and the source of my frustration.

The Universal Laws have been a topic of study and discussion for centuries. While learning these principles, I developed ideas that were new to the way I perceived the world, ideas that influenced the way I responded to different events and circumstances in my life. As I began to apply Universal Law philosophies to my own thinking, I noticed significant changes in that thinking. I was more peaceful, calm and clear-headed as I faced the challenges my life presented. I began to feel a drastically inflated sense of hope and motivation for the future. Past frustrations, which had been weighing me down, became learning opportunities that fueled me forward.

One major development in my new personal philosophy was a greater understanding of how we relate to the world around us. Everything we know or experience in life falls into three distinct categories or "Spheres": the Indirect Sphere, the Direct Sphere and the Action Sphere.

Each event and circumstance that we face has a certain nature that requires a different perspective and understanding to appreciate, respond to, and benefit from. All of the events in one Sphere can be thought of and dealt with in a particular way, while events from another Sphere require a different understanding and perspective. When we treat events and circumstances that occur in what I refer to as the Indirect Sphere as if they were in our Direct Sphere, we produce undo angst, fear and frustration. These unintended results rob us of the energy to pursue our ambitions and create a positive impact on the world around us. When we focus on the things in life that are outside our control, we miss opportunities to make the best of what we can personally influence and affect.

This idea that everything can be organized or categorized into one of three Spheres made the most significant alteration to my personal philosophy, as well as my ability to find reason and understanding while creating more peace, hope and happiness in my life. I now love things that I didn't before. I appreciate things I once loathed. Most importantly, I have greater control over my emotions and attitude than I ever have in the past. As a result, this reduction in stress and anxiety has literally changed my life. The person I was just a few years ago is but a shadow of the person I feel I am today.

This book began as a solitary activity in capturing my thoughts and ideas as I developed this evolving personal philosophy. Much of the content in this book was derived from my own journal, which followed me on a journey of pondering, reflecting upon, and testing these new theories in my own life. I found it very helpful to try to articulate my thoughts, while they were still fresh in my mind, into words that attempted to express the sometimes intangible feelings and developing concepts I experienced. The more I wrote, and the more I got from my readings and reflections, the more I learned from the lectures and seminars I attended. I found the act of writing created a new dimension to my reading and reflecting, one I had never experienced before; it provided an opportunity to better digest everything I knew. My journal grew into a series of writings that I thought might one day help me share these reflections with others—specifically my daughter. Those reflections, collected during many late nights, became the foundation of this and future books.

If these words can help someone find a little more peace or make greater sense of their life, I will be extremely grateful for this opportunity and privilege. The enormous effort to articulate my thoughts and ideas in order to create this book will have been worth every step of the process.

Still, I would be dishonest if I didn't admit that the greatest benefit of this project has been what I have gained in the process. The challenge of putting my thoughts into words, and being forced to digest and reflect on these ideas so thoroughly has been an experience in growth that is more than I could ever have asked for.

In this book, I have shared some ideas that will help you find a greater balance in your own life. I want to enable you with tools you can use to transmute the negative energy in your life and offload some of your stress.

There is more in this life that requires our time, energy, and attention than we could ever deal with effectively. This is why we must learn to direct our attention to the things that matter most—the things that will increase our positive energy, provide the greatest fulfillment and promote the positive impact we have on the lives of others.

I hope the ideas in this book will lighten your load, inspire more positive energy, build your hope and faith for success, and allow you to be more effective in the pursuit of your dreams.

It's time for you to begin your new journey...

Exercises

―――――――――――○―――――――――――

Section One: Write It Down

Remember, Week One of this exercise involved you rating every day with a number, 1 through 10, and listing out the events or circumstances that contributed to that days' number. If you have completed your Week One commitment, move on to Week Two.

Week Two: For this week, I want you to focus on three tasks with your journaling:

Resolve to use the power of at least one Law every day, and then actively seek out opportunities to do so. You do not need big tragedies to use the Laws to your benefit, to find positives from seemingly negative events. Even small frustrations can be alleviated to improve upon your day. (It might be helpful to carry your Universal Laws Quick Reference List to help you with this task.)

Write a number at the start of each page, 1 through 10, to reflect how good or bad your day was.

Below that, write a list of the Laws you reflected on throughout the day, including the circumstances involved and what results you experienced as you actively harnessed the power of that Law.

Week Three: That's right, there is a third week to this exercise if you choose, though you don't have to journal during this week (unless, of course, you choose to!).

During Week Three, I want you to compare your entries from week one and two. Average out your daily ratings for each week and reflect on your overall outlook and state of mind from one week to the next. Do you see a difference?

Usually, barring any unforeseen tragedies, it is clear that your second week, lived with intention and the Universal Laws in mind, was much more fruitful and positive overall.

Helpful Tip: I would encourage you to continue this journaling project, particularly if you were able to see a noticeable difference in your own vibration as a result!

Section Two: Name That Law

Scenario One

RAPHAEL IS THE FIRST member of his family to attend college. Paying his tuition has not been easy, and in order to take as few student loans out as possible, he works twenty hours a week, on top of keeping up with a full course load. There are days when he is exhausted and plenty of times when he misses out on social activities the rest of his peers are enjoying. But Raphael always has a smile on his face, and whenever anyone asks him how he does it all, he reminds them that the pot of gold at the end of this rainbow is that degree, which will not only help him get his dream job, but will also make his family so proud.

What Law is Raphael applying?

Answer: *Law of Gender.* Everything in life takes time to come to fruition. The most significant accomplishments often take the most time to cultivate.

Scenario Two

SANDRA WAS IN A CAR ACCIDENT on the way to work. She hit a patch of black ice, which caused her car to swerve into the vehicle driving in the next lane over. Both cars were badly damaged, but she and the other driver walked away with minimal injuries. Unfortunately, Sandra's insurance does not cover a rental vehicle, and she will be out her $500 deductible for repairs—a lot of money for her. She could be exceedingly frustrated and upset over this turn of events, but instead can't help but remember a similar accident she read about a year ago that proved fatal for one of the drivers. Rather than dwelling on the difficulties this accident now presents to her life, she is choosing to be thankful that both she and the other driver were safe and healthy after their wreck.

What Law is Sandra utilizing?

Answer: *Law of Relativity.* Her situation may appear bad at first, but when related to an alternate circumstance, she is very lucky and blessed to be alive and healthy.

Scenario Three

C HRIS AND EMILY MET as teenagers at an Al-Anon group for friends and family members of alcoholics. Both were in foster care as a result of their parents' abusive actions when drinking. Both were struggling with anger and feelings of depression over their circumstances and the tragic lives they had led up to this point. But through their friendship, as well as talking with to other teenagers in similar situations, they began to build upon a shared passion for helping children in foster care. They formed an advocacy group made up of current and former foster care youth in their area and began working toward reforms to improve the foster care experience. These reforms included playing a hand in increasing the age children could remain in foster care from 18 to 21. As adults, both Chris and Emily remained committed to making a difference for those still in foster care, and to empowering other children facing similar struggles as they once did.

What Law are Chris and Emily utilizing?

Answer: *Law of Transmutation.* What could have manifested as severe frustration and anger was used to motivate these two to a greater purpose helping to make a difference in the lives of others.

Section Three: Tactical Mission

Fictional examples of disrupted OODA Loops:

Romeo and Juliet: In the death scene, Romeo finds Juliet in the tomb and believes her to be dead, so he kills himself rather than live a life without her. The problem is, she wasn't dead—but when she wakes to find her lover's lifeless body beside her, she then kills herself as well. If Romeo had taken the time to Observe and Orient himself in the situation prior to Acting, he may have discovered Juliet was still barely breathing but very much alive.

Orange is the New Black: In the Season One finale, a conflict between Piper and fellow inmate Pennsatucky escalated when Pennsatucky followed Piper outside to confront her just as Piper was experiencing a bit of a breakdown. What followed highlights how the OODA Loop can be disrupted in times of distress. When Pennsatucky attacks and Piper realizes she is all alone with no one to help her, she goes to the extreme in defending herself, beating Pennsatucky quite severely in the midst of what seems to be a mental break. She went from Observe to Act and didn't seem to have the ability to process when to stop acting. Under less stressful circumstances, she probably would not have taken her own retaliation so far.

Resources

Also available by Garret Biss:

If you would like to learn more about the Universal Laws as discussed, be sure to check out garretbiss.com and look for future installments to the *A Life Unchained* series. *Charity The Gifts of Giving* is a book that discusses the many benefits that the donor receives when contributing to charity.

Acclaim for *Charity:*

"Biss does a terrific job of explaining the many ways that charity and selfless acts benefit BOTH the giver and the receiver."

– **Jack Canfield,** Co-creator, Chicken Soup for the Soul®

Be sure to visit http://garretbiss.com for the latest updates and to access additional resources.

Acknowledgements

———————————— ◎ ————————————

THANK YOU TO THE MANY FRIENDS and colleagues who offered their time to review drafts of this book and provide their invaluable feedback. This book wouldn't have been possible without your support: "Dutch," Sarah, Kristin, Elainia, "Prospect," "K.C.," Jennie, Dave, Lori, Blake, Nicolle, Lea, Dawn and many, many others.

It takes a village to raise a child and slightly less than a village to create a book. My most sincere thank you to the many with a hand in putting this book together—Jane, Heather, Leah, Diane, Toni, countless freelancers for various tasks, and of course... Mom, Dad, and D.

About The Author

G ARRET BISS was born and raised in Wilmington, Delaware. He enlisted in the United States Marine Corps in 1999, beginning a 16-year career of service to his country. During this time, he earned a Bachelor of Mechanical Engineering Degree at the University of Maryland, College Park, and a commission as an officer in the Marines. While on one of his most recent deployments, Garret was inspired to help others find meaning in their lives through writing and sharing his reflections about life, happiness, success and contribution. His passion for writing led to the publication of his first award-winning book, *Charity The Gifts of Giving*. *The Spheres Approach to Happiness and Life Fulfillment* marks Garret's fourth published book, with many yet to come.

Garret has had the great fortune to be mentored by the international best-selling author and visionary, Gary Keller (author of *The One Thing* and co-founder of Keller Williams). He has also been trained and supported by America's #1 Success Coach, Jack Canfield, (co-creator of Chicken Soup for the Soul and author of *The Success Principles*).

Garret is also the founder of the nonprofit One Million Goal, Inc., a foundation devoted to raising money and awareness to help provide water to those in need. Nearly 1 in 10 people on this planet live without access to clean drinking water. One Million Goal has joined the fight to help change that reality. This organization was aptly named for Garret's personal goal to help provide water to one million men, women and children in need.

In addition to being a published author, philanthropist and professional speaker, Garret has a Master of Real Estate Development degree from Auburn University. While considering his future in real estate development, Garret began reflecting on the differing cultures he had experienced in his travels with the Marines. Garret wanted to understand how past events and innovations have led to where we are as an American society regarding living conditions and societal standards, and to assess how that would affect an American society of the future. The result is a book entitled *Understanding the New America Dream: The Challenges and Benefits of New Urbanism*, which expresses his reflections and makes predictions about the future of America based on trends of today. While pursuing his degree, Garret received prestigious recognition as a Charles Grossman Scholarship recipient by the International Council of Shopping Centers (ICSC) Foundation.

In 2015, Garret retired from the Marine Corps as a Captain; he currently lives in New Bern, North Carolina where he spends time writing, reflecting and speaking to audiences of any size about living a more positive, abundant and fulfilling life—creating *A Life Unchained*.

32730199R00119

Made in the USA
Middletown, DE
15 June 2016